Wad-ja-get?

THE GRADING GAME
IN AMERICAN EDUCATION

Wad-ja-get?

THE GRADING GAME
IN AMERICAN EDUCATION

BY

Howard Kirschenbaum
ADIRONDACK MT. HUMANISTIC EDUCATION CENTER
UPPER JAY, NEW YORK

Rodney Napier
COLLEGE OF EDUCATION
TEMPLE UNIVERSITY

Sidney B. Simon
SCHOOL OF EDUCATION
UNIVERSITY OF MASSACHUSETTS

Hart Publishing Company, Inc. • *New York City*

Acknowledgements

Dr. Leland Howe, for his extremely helpful suggestions and editorial comments; Miss Sarah Engel for her research assistance; Miss Geraldine Ball, for her secretarial help; and to one 10th grade English class at Abington High School, one Political and Social Thought class at the New Lincoln School, and several Temple University values clarification courses, for actually living many of the incidents described on these pages.

Wad-ja-get?

Blow sois

THE GRADING GAME
IN AMERICAN EDUCATION

Contents

Wad-ja-get?

THE GRADING GAME
IN AMERICAN EDUCATION

Introduction

AMERICAN EDUCATION is in trouble.

Across the nation, the news of student strikes, boycotts, occupation of campus buildings, racial conflicts, destruction of school property and even the imprisonment of university officials has become commonplace. One exhaustive study determined that over 2,000 high schools underwent disruptions from November, 1968, to May, 1969.[1]

The issues in the student uprisings and protests are familiar, numerous and varied: humanize education, accept more black students, don't fire certain teachers, liberalize curfew rules in the dormitory, get better cafeteria food, rescind a recent disciplinary ruling, don't allow recruiters from Dow Chemical on campus, eliminate ROTC, offer a degree program in Afro-American studies, give students a role in the selection and tenuring of faculty, don't expand the university at the expense of the neighborhood residents who would lose their homes, fire a university president or teacher, eliminate caps and gowns at commencement exercises, allow free speech and political activity on campus, liberalize the dress regulations, and finally, among the many, many others, eliminate the traditional grading system.

Grading is one of the most controversial topics in American education. From the elementary to the graduate level, most of the student's or the teacher's life in school revolves, directly or indirectly, around the grading system. In recent years, the traditional grading system using *A*'s, *B*'s and *C*'s has come under increasing criticism. Thousands of schools have been beset by controversies concerning grading and evaluation. As a result, hundreds of schools and colleges have already introduced changes in their grading systems.

Is the traditional system of grading—the one most of us experienced throughout many years of schooling—*the most educationally useful system of evaluation?* This is the basic question that schools and colleges across the country have been grappling with.

In our attempt to formulate an answer to this question, we have tried to compile the most comprehensive survey of the history, research, alternatives and pro and con arguments about grading to date. Hoping to make the issues surrounding grading come alive—as they are actually experienced by millions of students and teachers every day—we have written this book in the form of a novel.

The drama at Mapleton High School is not really one story but a composite of events, personalities and documents drawn from many real sources.

We hope these pages will be of significant help to the many students, teachers, administrators and parents who

are concerned about finding new alternatives to one of
education's most persistent problems—"Wad-ja-Get?"

HOWARD KIRSCHENBAUM
RODNEY NAPIER
SIDNEY B. SIMON

AuSable Forks, New York
August, 1970

1 | *The First Debate: The Grading of Creativity*

AL HAYNES began passing out the papers. It wasn't long before the first murmurs could be heard.

"What? He *graded* them?" Leslie Johnson whispered to her friend, Stephanie.

"How can you grade *poetry?*" Jack Abrams mumbled from the back of the room.

"He's gotta be kidding," Barry Corlink groaned.

"Wad-ja-get, Leslie?" Stephanie asked.

After all the poems were returned to the students, the safety-in-numbers feeling grew, and reactions became more heated.

"That's the most ridiculous thing I ever heard of!"

"A *C*-minus. That's not fair!"

"How dumb can you get?"

Although it was his first year in teaching, Robert Jeffreys had taught long enough to know that the students' groans and "not fairs" were taking on an unusual intensity. He grew uncomfortable and started to fiddle with the attendance cards on his desk.

Finally he asked, "O.K. What's the matter?"

"You can't grade poetry," Jack Abrams said, after a pause.

"I *can't?*" Mr. Jeffreys queried. "I've graded everything else, and you haven't complained."

"But poetry's *different*," several students replied.

"Yeah. Mrs. Lindsay never used to grade our creative writing papers last year."

Mr. Jeffreys tried to comprehend what his students were saying, but he was having trouble.

"I don't understand," he said. "Why should poetry be treated differently? Some of your poems were thoughtful and contained some very skillful imagery; but others were full of cliches and seemed awkward and contrived. Now do you mean to tell me I can't legitimately give one poem a higher grade than another?"

"It's not that," Joe Pendleton said. "It's just that, well, what you think is a good poem, I might think is a bad poem. Or that a cliche to you might be a very original phrase to me. It's different in a composition. There you can pick out a spelling error or a punctuation error or a run-on sentence, so you can give the composition a grade. But just about anything goes in poetry."

Mr. Jeffreys inwardly groaned. *Anything goes in poetry* —talk about cliches! How could he make them see that poetry, too, had its form, its structure, its conventions, and that one *could* distinguish between an original image and a hackneyed one? On the other hand, Mr. Jeffreys wondered, what kind of grade would e.e. cummings have received on *his* poems in high school? Maybe that attempt at poetry Johnny Garrett handed in wasn't tripe at all. Maybe it did have an original style and meaning. Oh, that's nonsense. Of course it was trash.

"Look," he said to the class, trying to get out of this predicament, "personally, I think that poetry *can* be graded just like anything else. But I don't want to argue with you about it. If it will make you feel more comfortable, I won't grade your poetry from now on. O.K.? It's settled." His voice was flat, and tiredness showed in the lines around his mouth. It was Friday, and Jeffreys looked forward to the weekend.

"But wait! That's not fair either," said Susie McGill, one of the few students in the class who really was serious about poetry.

"Now what's wrong?" Mr. Jeffreys demanded, his impatience beginning to show.

"Well, poetry is one of the few things I like and do well. I always get low grades on formal compositions and on vocabulary tests and stuff like that, but I like poetry. So it's not fair to me if you don't grade poetry."

"Me, too," Seth Katzman chimed in. "I do better on creative writing assignments than on anything else. You'd be penalizing me if you didn't grade poetry."

"But how *can* you grade poetry?" Jack Abrams asked.

"Look, I agree with you," Susie said. "I don't think *anything* should be graded, *especially* poetry. But if you *don't* grade poetry and you grade everything else, it's unfair to the poets in the class."

The suggestion that there actually might be some poets in the class raised a few chuckles.

"Yeah," said Seth. "This is our strong area. We deserve to get good grades in it and have those grades pull up our average."

"But what about the rest of us?" asked Audrey Brown. "It's our *weak* area. Why should we be penalized because you *like* this stupid stuff?"

"Yeah. That's right," echoed several others.

"O.K., that's enough," said Mr. Jeffreys. "I don't think one side is going to convince the other, so we might as well not waste time repeating ourselves. Since most of the class seems to feel that poetry shouldn't be graded, I think we have to go with the majority—no grading on poetry."

Because Mr. Jeffreys' tenth grade English class would not get grades on their poetry assignments, the majority of the class liked Mr. Jeffreys a little more and felt a glow for the democratic process. A small minority were disgruntled. But it *was* Friday, and like Mr. Jeffreys, they, too, wanted the weekend to come quickly. The bell rang and the students stuffed their poems into their notebooks and went off to face the ordeals of geometry or biology or French II.

For a few of the students, however, the debate was not over. During 6th period lunch, while Seth Katzman was deciding which one of the two remaining desserts he should select, he was approached by Susie McGill.

"I hope you take the pie," Susie said, " 'cause I want the pudding." Although they had rarely spoken to each other in class, their apparent agreement in the morning's battle had made them almost friends.

"I don't know. Maybe we'll have to vote on it," Seth

said jokingly.

"I'm for grading all desserts!" Susie proclaimed.

"Well, you can't win 'em all," Seth said. They paid for their desserts and carried them to a table near the window.

"I'm still burning at the way Jeffreys went along with the majority, just to be a good guy," Susie said.

"Well, what do you expect? It's his first year teaching."

"Yeah, but why do *I* always have to get the new teachers?"

"You know what bothered me?" Seth said. "I've always been against grades. And I've really been against grading poetry. Yet, there I was, saying that our poetry should be graded."

"I know. Me too. But what could we do? To grade the regular stuff and not grade creative writing kind of means that creativity is less important than anything else we do in school."

"Yeah, but we sounded like we were in *favor* of grades."

"I know. And what really gets me is that I don't even believe that the kids who were saying that you can't grade poetry believed what they were saying. I think they were objecting simply because they got low grades on their poems. I noticed that the few kids who got *A's* weren't saying very much."

"Hey, you're right. Boy, that makes me mad. But what can we do about it?"

They both sat and thought for a while. Then Seth said,

"Look, you and I enjoy writing, right? So let's use our talent. Let's write something and see if we can't make a real issue out of this grading thing. I bet we could get it printed in the school paper!"

"That's a great idea, Seth. Look, this weekend think of as many arguments as you can to point out what's wrong with the grading system. I'll do the same. Then Monday during lunch we'll pool our ideas and work up something sensational."

"Will do. Sounds great. See you Monday."

The following week the two of them spent each lunch period working together. On Friday they submitted their effort to the *Mapleton High Herald* and eagerly awaited the reactions from both the faculty and the other students.

The *Herald,* like many high school newspapers, confined itself to a scrupulous absence of controversy. It was big on articles about statewide band contests, scholarships won by Mapleton students, and the rise and fall of the various athletic teams. Editorials on school spirit were a staple. In the midst of this blandness, Seth and Susie were sure their article would attract much attention.

Their article was published in the next issue of the *Herald,* exactly as they had written it:

SOMETHING'S WRONG WITH THE GRADING SYSTEM

In English class recently, we had a brief argument

as to whether or not poetry should be graded. The majority felt it should not be graded, and we agree. How can a school grade creativity and originality? Who is to decide what is creative or original? An original idea to one person might be a hackneyed idea to another person.

But let's face it. Everyone wants good grades and will do whatever he can to get them. If the school does not give grades for creativity, then students will not make any effort to be creative. They will spend their time and energy doing those things which *will* be rewarded.

The first criticism we have of grades is that they put the emphasis on the type of learning which can be graded easily. That is why we have so many multiple choice, fill-in, matching, and true-false tests—they're easy to grade. (They probably also take less time to grade.) But what does this do to our education? For the convenience of the teachers who are forced to grade us, the more important aspects of our education—the ones which are not easy to grade—are neglected.

Grades also turn students into a bunch of robots. We do whatever teachers want us to do, even if we know that what we are being required to do is only "busy work," and even if we think such work is only a waste of time. The fact is, we're scared of many of our teachers because of the power that grading gives them over us.

Thirdly, we do not feel that grades are fair. For example, if one student has trouble in French and works hard at it and gets a *C*, and another student finds French easy and doesn't work at it and gets a *B*, is that fair? If a student really tries hard in a subject and gets a low grade, he might get discouraged and stop trying. We've seen this happen to some of our classmates. So grading isn't fair to kids who have trouble in school but who really try hard. Teachers sometimes say they take effort into account, but how do they know how hard we have worked on something? And how do they know how hard it was for us to do a particular assignment? How can a teacher really be fair when he or she has 130 students to grade?

Finally, we're against grading because it encourages cheating. From what we've seen, most people in this school cheat, in one way or another. How can we pretend this is a good school if so many people care so little about their education that they are willing to cheat their way through it?

Maybe it's time we thought about the problems that grading creates. We think this would be a much better school if marks were completely eliminated.

2 | *An Introduction to Mapleton High School: Three Viewpoints*

THE DAY had a blue calm to it. No wind stirred. The streets were dry, and the hills were still dotted with patches of snow—the last traces of winter. A man in his early forties sat in the hard-top convertible belonging to Rip Wilson, one of Mapleton's most popular real estate brokers. They had left Wilson's office and were driving north toward the Hidden Hills section of town.

"So you're going to work with Bowman's Insurance firm, are you? Well, you couldn't have picked a better community to move to. I grew up in Mapleton. I don't want to give my age away, but I played football for Mapleton on the team that won the state championship back in, well, let's say the 40's—*late* 40's." He laughed. "Well, anyway, it was a hell of a team!"

"And you've lived here all of your life, Mr. Wilson?" the man asked, looking at the houses as they drove along.

"You got it! Outside of a little time over in Asia fighting for the flag, I've been right here in Mapleton. Yes, sir, this is a good town. The people are decent and hard-working. The town's growing, too—more and more people moving out of the city, just like everywhere else in this country. When they put the electronics plant out here, things really boomed. Don't get me wrong; I'm not complaining or anything. I've sold a lot of houses in the last ten years. The electronics guys could afford expensive ones, so the prices went up on everything we had around here. And with the increased tax base, we could put up our new high school. That's it. Over there on your right. It's a pretty damn impressive place, huh?"

"It certainly is. My two kids will be going there you know. We all went over to see the building last week. The kids couldn't believe how different it looked from their school in the city. The glass walls, all the grounds and playing fields . . . "

"And the *inside!* Boy, isn't that something? It sure is different from the Mapleton High *I* went to. They've got these regular-sized classrooms, and small classrooms for discussion groups, I guess, and some rooms that must seat, oh, at least a hundred and fifty kids. Then they have those sliding doors, so they can put two classrooms together. I'll tell you, things sure are changing. I don't know. I sometimes think that *we* turned out all right, and we didn't have a five million dollar school to go to. But that's progress, I guess," Wilson said.

They were driving by the shopping center now. They passed Sears, the Lerner's dress shop, Burt's shoe store, the Rexall drug store, the Grand Union supermarket and many others. Wilson pointed out how accessible the shopping center was to the house they were going to see. "Why you could practically walk it on a nice day," he said.

"Yes, that's good," the passenger said.

"And I might add that out here, people aren't *scared* to do a little walking. Our streets are safe."

His passenger looked at Wilson questioningly. The broker went on.

"Yes, sir, you don't have to worry about *that* out *here*. I'm proud to say we have no race problem in Mapleton. Our colored families fit right in with everyone else. We even have one or two colored *doctors*. They all live over in Ritter Park, on the other side of town. We get along fine."

"What percentage of the population is black, would you say?"

"Well, I don't think I know offhand, but I seem to remember, let's see, there are 2,400 kids at Mapleton and about 200 Negroes. So what does that make it, about 8%?"

"I see."

"Yes, sir, we're pretty well-integrated out here. We've got about 40% Protestant, 30% Catholic and 30% Jewish. Of course, a lot of the Catholic children go to the parochial school. I can't see why, really. I mean, we've probably got the best school system around here. But I guess you already know that."

"Yes, as I mentioned, the high school was one of the first places we checked on in Mapleton. It's a very impressive school. And I liked the principal; he was very nice to us, very helpful."

"Oh, sure. Joe Cunningham. He's a good man. He runs a pretty tight ship over there; although, I'll tell you, I can't say as I agree with everything that goes on there. I mean all the money they spend. You know they have closed-circuit television and a special study center for each department? When I went to school, we had one big study hall in the auditorium, or else you did your homework at home. In that new building, the kids can do their homework in a half dozen' different places. Now *that's* a waste of good money, if you ask me.

"But I can't complain. Over 60% of the kids go on to college, and we always have a few who get into those big schools—you know, like Harvard. Why I read in the paper just last week that our kids are in the top ten percent of the nation on some test they give to everybody. I guess Cunningham must know what he's doing.

"I'll tell you one thing, he's a good politician. He knows how to please almost everybody—both the radicals and the conservatives, and let me tell you, we've got plenty of both out here. But the kids haven't demonstrated or boycotted or any of that stuff you read about, so people out here are pretty happy with the schools. Well, here we are—one-twelve Sparrows' Lane. I think you'll like this place."

> As we bid a fond farewell to teachers and friends we have known during our four happy and busy years here at Mapleton, our hearts are filled with joy and sorrow.
>
> These have been important years. Years of growth and maturity and discovery and excitement. Yes, and occasionally, of pain and tears. For Mapleton has

been our life, and life will always be a mixture of happiness and sadness.

We've learned about life at Mapleton High. We know that Mapleton High tried to give us a relevant education. Our teachers have brought the real world into our classrooms. We students fought for and won the right for boys to wear sideburns and for girls to wear slacks on cold, winter days. Our class headed the drive to raise money for a Peace Corps school in Peru. And we led the march to the Courthouse for equal voting rights in Mississippi.

Our minds are flooded with the joyous memories of our years at Mapleton. Who will ever forget the trip to Washington? Or the water balloon that almost got Mr. Harper? Would he ever have forgiven us if it had really bombed him? Who will ever forget the play-off and Johnny Chiminsky's sinking two out of two foul shots to tie the score and send us into overtime? Who will ever forget the Christmas pageant when Jerry Kelly's Magi beard fell off, becoming an extra gift to the Christ child?

These and other memories are captured in the following pages. May this yearbook not mark the end of our education, but rather the beginning. We look forward to our 10th reunion when we can all meet again and see what life has brought to each of us: May the next ten years be even one tenth as happy as these four years at Mapleton have been for all of us. Peace.

The Yearbook Staff

Dear Danny,

Well, you're going to get the last laugh after all.

Last year before we graduated, I thought I'd done so much better than you when I landed this job at Mapleton and you had to settle for that little two-by-nothing junior high in the middle of nowhere. Well, as it turns out, you're enjoying yourself out there, and I've decided to leave here.

I've come to the conclusion that this school is a big facade. The level of teaching here falls far short of what you'd expect in this fancy building. For example, the physical structure of the building and the innovative modular scheduling system are arranged to allow students to work independently in a dozen different locations throughout the building. All very modern, right? Well, get this: The teachers are *still* assigning "Chapter 4 and the questions at the end" for homework. These kids can use the library (Instructional Materials Center, it's called here), the reading room, any one of seven departmental study centers, the student lounge, or the study hall for their homework. Big deal! It's still "Chapter 4 and the questions at the end."

As far as I can tell, the problem seems to be the way most teachers were taught and the way they were trained to teach. It will probably be years before teachers are trained to "individualize instruction," which is what these new buildings were designed for.

The principal is O.K.—not a particularly inspiring leader, but he'll go along with any well-thought-out idea you have, as long as it doesn't rock the boat too much. But it's obvious he's dragging a faculty behind him who would just as soon not be bothered with anything new. I don't mean that all of the teachers here at Mapleton are old-fashioned and incompetent.

We have young teachers, old teachers and middle-aged teachers—some good, some bad and some mediocre. I suppose on the average they're a lot better than most. Most of the teachers have their Master's degrees, and the average is nine years' teaching experience.

And the students? Typical. In all the classes, even the honors classes, very few of the students ever get enthusiastic. Groans and protests invariably follow any major assignment. The students don't seem to have any genuine respect for their teachers. Oh, they're polite enough to us, and serious discipline problems are rare, but the kids tell me they regard most of their teachers as very unimportant figures in their lives, as adults who have nothing "really important" to teach them. Most students here seem to view their teachers as purveyors of subject matter—occasionally interesting, but usually boring and "irrelevant"—not as human beings with whom it is possible to have meaningful interaction.

I think Mapleton fits the all-too-familiar pattern of the school in which students are apathetically going through the motions of getting an education, passing through a series of prescribed hurdles to get a diploma —that necessary ticket of admission to society's benefits. The students feel compelled to perform tasks not of their choosing and not to their liking. I've tried to make my own English class more meaningful for the kids, and they seem to have responded favorably to my approach, but I don't know. I feel pretty isolated in the department. I feel that now I'm ready to go on for my Master's, so I have decided to make the move.

This school has a lot of contradictions. In some

ways Mapleton is among the best and most modern schools in the country. The students and the graduates bring honor to the school both scholastically and athletically. The building is in the forefront of architectural design in education. This community is wealthy enough to afford a teaching staff which is both experienced and, theoretically, capable of effecting a really exciting program. I say "theoretically" and that's what gets me. All the ingredients are here for each student to receive the best education possible, and yet nothing changes. Same old methods; same old theories. As far as I'm concerned, the school's a *sham*. For the kids' sake, I hope somebody does something to shake things up around here.

Let me know if you hear of any good openings. I've got one job offer in the city, but I'm not sure I want to take it.

See you soon, I hope.

Jack

3 | *Mr. Cannon's Class*
Argues about Grades

FRIDAY, OCTOBER 24TH was a brilliant, musky, exhilarating autumn day. The downpour the night before had washed the sky clear. This was football weather—a day for even the most apathetic student to be glad he was alive.

Walter Cannon's third period, 11th grade American history class filed into the room with more than their usual good spirits. Someone was enthusiastically whistling the Beatle's new song. One of the boys put the punch line of a joke just out of Cannon's earshot, but the laughter from his friends welled in through the door ahead of them.

"Hey, Mr. Cannon, where'd you get that tie?" Terry Hansen asked. "Was there a fire sale at your neighborhood Salvation Army?"

"As a matter of fact, it was a gift from Calvin Coolidge to my mother on the day I was born. President Coolidge bought it at a Vermont auction in 1925 and saved it for me." Mr. Cannon delivered his answer with a straight face.

The students liked Walter Cannon. In his eight years of teaching at Mapleton High, he had earned the reputation for being strict, but also human. The students knew they had to work for Cannon and that their work had to be of high quality as well. But the students knew they could talk to him. At 32 he was young enough to listen to and understand their problems and yet old enough to offer help and objectivity. When he was wrong, he would admit it, even in front of the whole class. This rare quality earned him the trust and the respect of his students.

Friday was current events day in Mr. Cannon's classes. He believed that students could learn a lot from each other. Sometimes he started off the discussion; sometimes the topic came from one of the students.

"Well, does anyone have anything he'd like to raise for discussion this morning?" Cannon asked.

"There's an article I read in the *Times* science section," Leroy Aimes said. "It was about this new cancer cure."

"Do you think we could use it for the topic of discussion this morning, Leroy?"

"Well, I don't know. It is pretty interesting. You know, cancer and all."

"O.K. How many people would like to hear about this new research on cancer and then perhaps discuss it?"

Three or four students raised their hands.

"Oh, well," Cannon said, gently. "I guess that topic doesn't grab too many people. Maybe you few could meet Leroy for lunch today and discuss it . . . Does any-one else have a suggestion?"

"I do," Betty Stone replied. "Did anyone read the article in our *Herald* about grades? That would make a good discussion topic."

A few of the students who had read the article immediately voiced their agreement.

"How many of you read this article?" asked Cannon, who had had to tackle a long-delayed stack of student papers the night before and, therefore, hadn't seen the most recent issue of the *Herald*.

About a third of the class raised their hands.

"I have a copy of the paper here," Jane Southern said. "Should I read the article?"

After Jane read Susie McGill's and Seth Katzman's article to the class, the arguments began flying back and forth.

"They're right. I'd be much more relaxed in school without grades."

"You'd be relaxed all right. You wouldn't do *any* work."

"Speak for yourself. *You're* the one who works for grades like they're going out of style, not *me*. . ."

"I disagree with their point that grades aren't fair for the kid who tries hard but who just doesn't have what it takes. For example, if everyone who tried hard got *A*'s, then you could have a real dummy graduating from here with an *A* average just because he tried hard. On the other hand, you might have someone who was a lot smarter, but who didn't try as hard, graduating with a *B* average. With only his *B* average the smarter kid does not get accepted into a first-rate college, whereas the dumber kid does get into the better college, but he can't do the work because it's too hard. Now does that make sense?"

"No, that doesn't make sense. But does it make sense to take a kid who has trouble in school and give that kid *D*'s and *F*'s? Maybe with additional help and more effort on his part, the kid could probably make it; but with the bad marks staring him in the face, he's so discouraged that he just stops trying. Does *that* make sense?"

"I hate school because of grades."

"You hate school because you get *low* grades."

"Well, *I* get high grades, and I hate grades too. I know it's stupid, but it's really important to me whether I get an 88 or a 91 or a 94. I'm never relaxed in school because I'm always fighting for grades."

"That's your problem; it's not the fault of grades. I get pretty good grades, but I'm relaxed about school."

"Can you imagine what would happen if grades were eliminated? Nobody would do any work. I know *I* wouldn't."

"How do you know? Have you ever been in that kind of a situation?"

"No, but I know myself well enough to know that I'd goof off. I'd never open my *math* book, that's for certain."

"Just listen to what you're saying. Do you mean that the reason we need grades is to force people to do work they ordinarily wouldn't do?"

"I disagree. I took a summer course in acting last summer. There were no grades, no credit even; but we all worked overtime at it. And I learned more than I've ever learned in a course where I *had* to work."

"But, you're assuming the courses are interesting. Let's face it—most of our courses are so boring that if you didn't get graded, you'd do only enough work to get by. It would be different if the courses were interesting."

Mr. Cannon brought up another question: "What about this section in the article on cheating? They say 'most people in this school cheat.' Most means 51% or more. Is that so? I know there is some cheating, but do you agree that there is *that* much?"

"I think there is," Jerry Szymanski said. "I know that in my French class at least half the kids cheat because Madame Graham is half blind."

The class laughed.

"Let's carry on this discussion without names, please," Cannon said sternly.

"I think the point's exaggerated. I suppose everyone cheats now and then, but most of the time they don't."

"Of course they don't most of the time," Barry Binson answered. "Most of the time they can't get away with it. And sometimes they don't need to cheat. But when a person *needs* to cheat and he *has* the opportunity, chances are he's going to cheat."

"How do *you* know?"

"Wait a minute," interrupted Cannon. "Maybe we

can get some facts to go on from this class, that is, if you'll be honest. For instance, if I asked how many of you cheated at least once last year, would you answer that?"

"Do you want us to raise our hands?"

"Well, what do you think? Would you be more comfortable if you wrote your answer down and handed it in without your name?"

The class like this idea, but when little slips of paper were handed out, they began to have some problem with what was considered cheating.

"What's cheating?" Joey Masters asked. "Copying someone's homework?"

"Good question," Cannon stated. "I guess that would be cheating in the sense that it's 'illegal.' But maybe we had better get all the varieties of cheating up on the board, to be sure we agree on our definition. So what other kinds of cheating are there?"

"Copying off someone else's test paper."

"O.K., that's an obvious example. What else?"

"Whispering an answer to someone."

"Copying long passages from encyclopedias or books for use in your term paper, and then hoping to pass them off as your own ideas."

"Using an old paper of your older brother and handing it in as your own."

"Using one of your own old papers."

"Making up footnotes and bibliographies of books that you didn't read . . . or that don't even exist."

The class laughed.

"Apparently some of you are familiar with that one," said Cannon, and the class laughed again.

"What about brown-nosing teachers for a better grade?" someone asked. "Isn't that a form of cheating?"

"Hmm. I think maybe that's a whole other category. Let's stick to the ones that we generally agree are 'illegal,' that you could get into trouble for if you got caught."

"Looking in the teacher's desk to find a copy of tomorrow's exam."

"Bringing in the answers to exams on crib sheets."

"Peeking in your book during a test."

"O.K.," said Cannon. "I guess that's enough to convey the idea of what cheating is, or what we mean by it, anyway. So take a minute to think about whether or not you did any of these last year, and if you did, write a 'yes' on your paper, and if you didn't, write a 'no' and pass them up. No names, please."

As it turned out, twenty of the twenty-eight students wrote "yes" on their papers.

"Well, if this is any indication of the rest of the school, I guess Susie's and Seth's point that most people cheat is an accurate one."

Inwardly, Cannon felt shocked at the results of this informal poll, although he tried not to show it. He did make a mental note to look up some research on cheating the first chance he got.

One student spoke up and denied that the results of

the poll were as significant as they seemed.

"Just because someone copies someone's homework once or twice, that doesn't mean he's really a cheater. When you say that 20 out of 28 kids cheat, that's misleading. It's just an occasional thing, except for a few hard-core cheaters."

But Terry Hansen disagreed.

"Someone said before that most of the time people don't cheat because they're afraid of getting caught. I think the point is that we *feel* that there is cheating going on all around us. And a lot of the time there *really is*. But what is more important than how many people cheat, and how often, is the *atmosphere* that's created by cheating. When I write a really good paper, I'm always worried the teacher will think I've copied it from a book. When I take a test and I look up and my eyes happen to meet the teacher's, I get worried that she'll think I've been looking at other people's papers, so I have to play all sorts of ridiculous games with my eyes and face to make it obvious that I'm just taking a stretch. And when I take a test, I have to keep my paper covered so I'm not accused of helping someone else. And teachers always seem so suspicious. 'Keep your eyes on your own paper.' 'Cover your answers.' 'No roving eyes.' 'Everybody do his own work.' How many times have you heard those? They police us like we're a bunch of convicts. You'd think we all had intentions of cheating all the time. That's the *feeling* you get."

Many heads nodded in support. A familiar chord in

the experience of most of the students had obviously been sounded. The discussion became much more serious and thoughtful.

"I sometimes feel that the only thing I really care about in school is what grades I get, and not how much I'm learning," Maria Rivera said.

"If I pull a bad report card, I'm really scared to go home," Jerry Symanski confessed. "I always think my father's gonna kill me."

"There was one class I had," said Betty Stone, "which I really liked. The teacher and I also got along fine. Then when I got my final grade, I felt it was really unfair, but the teacher wouldn't change it. So now I really have negative feelings about that class, even though I liked it."

After a while, one student asked, "Why do we have grades anyway?"

This deceptively simple question seemed to capture the class' interest, and they began offering different reasons for the existence of grades.

"Like I said before," said Sandy Farrell, "they need grades to get us to do boring work that we'd never *dream* of doing on our own."

"I heard it was to encourage us to do our best work," said Bill Forest. "I know I wouldn't put out very much in English if I wasn't worried about grades."

"I don't know whether grades have anything to do with our education at all. Maybe we have them because the colleges need grades as a basis for accepting students."

"Grades are needed to maintain discipline around here. Teachers can keep us in line easier when they can use the grade as a threat."

"If you get a bad grade in a subject, then you know you're not good in that subject."

"You're all wrong. You're all assuming that there *is* a logical reason for grades. It seems we've always had grades, and it's just tradition that keeps them going, like some bad habit."

"How do you know? There must have been some reason why they were first invented."

"Mr. Cannon, do you know why we have grades?"

All heads turned to the teacher, now placed in the role of giver of truth, answerer of questions, settler of all disputes.

Walter Cannon had a background in the Dewey-Kilpatrick progressive school of education. He believed that more important than an answer to a question was the process of finding the answer, of solving the problem. He also believed that students, working independently and in small groups, should be responsible for a major part of their learning. Philosophy aside, Walter Cannon simply did not know the answer to the question his students were asking.

"To tell the truth, I don't know," he said. "There's some logic to *all* your hypotheses. But I just don't know which ones, if any, are true."

The class seemed at a loss. Cannon was watching them closely. One of his favorite teaching techniques was to capitalize on student interest in the building of curriculum. He was thinking this might be a good time for some group planning.

He wrote the following questions on the blackboard:

1. Did we always have grades?
2. If we didn't, when were they introduced?
3. At what level of the educational system? Why?

"Did we always have grades? If we didn't, when were they introduced? At what level of the educational system? Why?"

Then he turned to the class and said, "Do these questions interest you at all?"

There was a pause; it was a hard question to answer immediately.

Finally Terry Hansen said, "Well, it's not as if I'm going to die if I don't find out the answers, but, yeah, they *do* interest me. I mean grades are so important to us in school. I'd really like to know why we have them and if there are any good reasons for using them."

Several of the other students agreed that Terry had summed up their feelings pretty accurately.

"Well," said Cannon, "I think this *would* be an interesting topic to explore. Since we are coming to the end of our unit on the Constitution and the Supreme

Court and will soon be starting another unit, what about exploring the history of American education, with a special emphasis on the history of grades? How does that sound?"

The class liked the idea. They selected several topics and periods that different committees should investigate and then divided themselves into those committees. One committee was given the specific focus of "the history of grades," but all of the committees were to be on the lookout for any relevant information on this subject. For example, if the committee on "the history of higher education before the Revolution" happened to find something on grading, they were to pass it along to the "history of grades" committee.

Two periods a week for the next two weeks would be allotted for the committees to meet and plan their reports. Outside of that, the work would have to be done on their own time. The reports were due the week of November 17th.

With growing enthusiasm, Cannon's third period history class went to work.

4 | *The Class Reports*
on the History of Grading

TERRY HANSEN was appointed chairman by the other four members of the "history of grades" committee. Since Terry was on the basketball team and the practice season was just beginning, he wouldn't have much time for research. But because he was an articulate writer and speaker, the committee gave him the job of combining all their information into one paper and presenting it to the class. The other members worked diligently on their individual reports, going to the library and tracking down as many articles and references on the history of grades as they could find.

On Tuesday of the week before Thanksgiving, the committee was scheduled to present its report. Terry served as moderator and explained the format of their presentation.

"Mr. Cannon, members of the third period American history class, and honored guests (wherever you are)," Terry began, to his classmates' amusement. "No, seriously, our report is going to be different from the last two you have heard. Instead of each of us reading a section of the whole report, I'm going to read the whole thing."

Again the class laughed, and Terry did too.

"No, you guys don't understand. *They* did all the leg work for this report; I just put together the results. I will read the report slowly, and whenever you want to, ask a question; one of the panel here will answer it. Get the idea?"

Apparently the class got the idea, because after looking around, Terry smoothed out his papers on Mr. Cannon's desk and began to read:

INTRODUCTION

We study, we produce and we get graded. It's the name of the game. We take it for granted. Grades are as familiar to us as apple pie, war, inflation, Monopoly and Post Office. As far as we knew, grades were invented along with schools. We've always had them, right?

Wrong! We haven't always had grades. In fact, they are quite a new innovation in the history of education. One of the startling things we discovered in doing this report was that almost nothing was written about grades before the 1900's.

What did exist before grades? When did grades come into use and why? What has been their history since they were introduced? These are the questions we intend to answer in our report.

Terry looked up from his paper. "Any questions?" he asked.

"How could we have any questions?" asked Terry's friend Joey Masters. "You haven't said anything yet." Some people, including Mr. Cannon who was sitting in the back of the room, laughed, and Terry gave Joey a mock dirty look and continued.

THE ANCIENT HISTORY OF GRADES

In the beginning all education took place within the family or social class unit. Performance was all that counted. To be an *A* hunter you killed the most game. To be an *A* farmer you harvested the most wheat. The product was readily visible, and success or failure was easy to measure. In ancient Sparta, the child's first test came at birth when a council of elders determined how fit he was to become a future citizen and warrior. To be scrawny or otherwise unfit resulted in the male child's being exposed to the elements until he died (a sure *F*). If he survived this first "pass-fail" examination, at the age of eight he received special instruction to become a courageous warrior. Again, the criteria for success were easy to judge. To run swiftly, to wrestle, to box, to use the shield and spear could be judged partly by immediate results in tested performance and partly by mere survival.

In the more cultured class of ancient Athens, formal education included subjects such as grammar and music. Evaluation was made on the basis of your skill in memorizing the wisdom of your teacher. To remember the *Iliad* was to *remember* the *Iliad*. Mastering this task was relevant to the needs of a boy at that time . . .

"Are you kidding me?" Jane Southern asked. "We read the *Iliad* in the ninth grade, and you mean to tell me that people then thought that was *relevant?*"

Terry called on Sandy Farrell, one of the panel members, to answer Jane.

"Sure it was relevant. Remember, much of what the Greeks believed, or said they believed, about religion, politics, warfare, history and so on, came from the *Iliad* and some other books like that. If you were going to be a community leader, you had to be able to quote passages from the *Iliad* and know the contents backwards and forwards. It's a little like quoting the *New York Times* and *Newsweek* today."

"So what does this have to do with grading?" Jane asked.

Sandy answered again. "Just this: The early teachers didn't grade their students. The student's particular competence, or lack of it, was readily apparent when he entered a public debate, or when he ran for political office, or when he was in physical combat."

"O.K.?" asked Terry. Since no one seemed to have anything else to say, he continued:

In the Middle Ages and the Renaissance, there was no need for grades either. In the homes, mothers passed their knowledge on to their daughters; the fathers, to their sons. If a boy wanted to learn a trade and join a guild, he studied with a Master until he was deemed ready to join the guild. If he wanted to enter the medieval universities and become a priest or churchman, he'd have to be examined, but as with masons or carpenters, what he had to do to pass was clear. There were no grades; you either passed or failed. Either you could do it, or you couldn't.

GRADES IN EARLY AMERICA

Just as in Greek and Roman days and in medieval and Renaissance times, only the children of the wealthy got a good education in early America. In fact, it wasn't until the mid-19th century, in both the United States and Europe, that education became widespread.

Frequently, these rich children had their own private tutors or else went to schools for children like themselves. The purposes of their tutoring and of these schools was to prepare for entrance into the famous colleges, like Harvard, William and Mary, and Yale. The student's knowledge was tested, often by use of examinations, but this was not for the purpose of giving grades.

"Then how could the colleges know which students to take if they didn't get grades?"

Barry Binson answered this time.

"Remember, in those days there wasn't a rat-race to get into college. Only a very select few went to school. Most boys then were needed to help in the fields or work in the factories to support their families. Anyone who could afford to, and who wasn't a complete numbskull, got into college."

"Provided you weren't a Negro or a woman," Maria Rivera called out. She had learned some things about discrimination in education while working on *her* committee's report.

"Unfortunately, Maria, that's true," Terry said and then picked up where he had left off.

> The purpose of this testing was two-fold: it demonstrated the student's progress, and it gave the teacher a clearer indication of what subjects required additional instruction to enable the student to handle the work required in college.

GRADES IN THE MID-19th CENTURY

In the middle of the 1800's, when government-supported elementary schools began to be popular, there was pressure to differentiate students. However, until about 1850, most elementary schools in the United States were of the one-room variety. Students of all ages and experience were grouped together under one teacher [1] and most students never got beyond elementary school. As the number of students increased, schools gradually became graded according to age level; and new ideas about curriculum and teaching methods were tried.[2] Famous educators, such as Pestalozzi and Herbart, began to describe teaching as an art.

The schools didn't have complex subject contents. The subjects were usually penmanship, arithmetic, writing, reading, history and, possibly, geography. Generally, the students showed their competencies by reading, writing and reciting. Progress evaluations were mostly descriptive, that is, the teacher would write down which skills the student could or couldn't do. This was done mostly for the student's benefit, since he would not move to his next subject area until he had mastered the previous one.

Changes came very slowly. Although elementary schools were more widely available, most children were still needed in the fields, factories and homes. After 1850, the number of students being educated increased from 13% to 20% within a period of 20 years.

THE LAST QUARTER OF THE CENTURY

The number of students entering public high schools increased rapidly with the passage of compulsory attendance laws at the elementary level. Between 1870 and 1910, the number of public high schools increased from 500 to 10,000; the total number of pupils in public elementary and high schools rose from 6,871,-000 to 17,813,000.[3] Subject areas in the high schools also became increasingly more specific.

Even though the elementary schools continued to employ written descriptions when evaluating each student's skills, the high schools began using percentages or other similar markings to measure the student's abilities in the different subject areas. In a sense, this was the beginning of grading as we know it today.

"How come they started with grades here?" Bill Forest asked.

"I'm just coming to that, Bill," Terry said.

Grading then was used basically to let students know how their own level of performance compared with the others' in the class. Usually an employer looked at a person's graduation certificate and considered the recommendations from teachers or other adults who were familiar with the student's abilities and character. The grades were not important.

However, as more and more students graduated from high school and wanted to get into college, and as more and more families could afford to send their children to college, the need to distinguish between all the high school graduates increased. So, one of the reasons grading was introduced was to help colleges screen their applicants.

A second reason was to help the teachers differentiate among students of varying abilities. The high schools were becoming bigger and could accomodate just about any elementary school graduate, so the teachers used grades to distinguish the faster from the slower students, with the hope that this would help their teaching.

By the turn of the century, percentage grading became increasingly popular, especially at the secondary school level. But many elementary and high schools were still getting along without any grading, or with just a few symbols, like S for satisfactory and U for unsatisfactory.

"Terry, before you go on, I'd like to make a point here," said Betty Stone, another member of the committee.

"Sure, Betty."

"Well, I think it's important to point out that although grading, as we know it today, was started during this time, the reason for grading was not an educational one. What I mean is, grading only helped the colleges in their selections of students and only helped teachers identify their students more easily. Nowhere was it argued, at least not in anything I've read, that grades were good for the *kids,* that they would help a kid's *education.* That's all I wanted to say."

"Good point, Betty. Thanks. Does anyone else have anything they'd like to say before I go on?"

"Yeah," Ed Hecht said. "I'd like to say I think this is pretty interesting. Could you go a little more slowly so I can jot down more notes?"

"Sure, Ed. And thanks for the compliment. Maybe it'll help our grade!"

Most of the class laughed and looked back toward Mr. Cannon. He just smiled back at them and didn't say anything. So their attention moved back to Terry.

So it came to pass that imperfectly educated teachers, using imperfect measures and imperfect criteria, began to grade students on subject matters that may or may not have had any obvious significance in the life of the student. Success was no longer measured in competitive debate, or in the sports arena or on the battlefield, or on the job. It was determined by the whim of the teacher in the classroom.

At one time in history, it was *the teacher* who was graded on the basis of the performance of his students. If a teacher's students succeeded in the competition of daily living, he was assured of more pupils and also a flourishing practice. But if his pupils consistently failed, he would not make it as a teacher and would probably have to get another job. Thus, in the earlier periods of education, the criteria of success were highly visible, and the teacher was, in many ways, held accountable.

But grading changed all that. Instead of success being judged by society once the student was out of school, success was now being judged by the teacher in the classroom. Thus, the teacher's evaluation became the focus of the learning experience rather than the student's preparation for life in the real world. Grading also took the teacher off the hook—no longer could he be held accountable for a student's failure. He would just point to the student's low marks.

THE BEGINNING OF CONTROVERSY: 1910-1920

Although American educators were not completely satisfied with the grading practices before 1910, there had been no major source of controversy. Things seemed to change gradually, and only a few people questioned the drift toward grading. In 1912, however, a study was conducted by Starch and Elliot which dramatically questioned the reliability of grades as a measurement of pupil accomplishment.[4]

The aim of the study was to determine how much the personal values and expectations of individual teachers influence their grading standards. To do this, copies of two English language examination papers, written by two pupils at the end of their first year in a large mid-west high school, were duplicated in their original form and sent to two hundred high schools. The principal teachers who taught first year English in each of the schools were asked to mark the papers according to the practices and standards of the school. One hundred forty-two schools returned their graded papers.

The papers were graded on the basis of 75 as a passing score. (At this time it was common practice to grade papers in terms of a percentage score based on an absolute score of 100.) For one paper, scores varied from 64 to 98 points, with an average of 88.2. The other paper had a range from 50 to 97, with an average score of 80.2.

In addition to purely subjective feelings which a teacher may have had concerning what makes a good paper (what sounds or feels good), some teachers highly valued neatness, spelling and punctuation; others focused primarily on how well the message was communicated. With more than thirty different scores for a single paper and a range of over forty points, there is little reason to wonder why the report of these results caused a "slight" stir among educators.

This study also caused a slight stir among Cannon's students. "What? A difference of 47 points? I can't believe it."

"I always knew the grading system was cock-eyed!"

"I figured that most teachers grade differently, but I didn't figure *that* differently."

"Those were English papers," Joey Masters said. "I can see where grading would be more subjective there. But what about science or math papers, for example?

Would the results be the same?"

Terry answered, "It seems to me I remember there was a study like that. Do one of you . . . ?"

"Yes," Betty Stone said, "I have the figures right here. We were going to include them, but we figured the report would be too long. As it turned out, a lot of people asked Starch and Elliot the same question Joey just asked, so they repeated the study using a geometry paper but doing everything else the same way.[5] Believe it or not, the results on this experiment showed an even *bigger* span in the grading.

"I'm not kidding. The figures are right here. From the 138 returns, the range on one paper was 67 points, with one teacher scoring the paper 28% and another teacher, 95%; 75% was the passing mark. While some teachers deducted points for only a wrong answer, many other teachers took neatness, form and spelling into consideration."

"So you can just imagine the controversy which arose," Terry said.

Questions which for years had been bothering educators concerning the grading process now began to surface, and efforts were made to correct some of the problems which existed. Particularly disturbing was the fact that in the Starch and Elliot study of the English papers, one boy was failed by 15% of the teachers grading his paper (his own teacher had given him an 80), while 12% of the teachers gave the same paper a grade of more than 90 points. Starch and Elliot found that chance alone could account for as much as a seven point difference between two teachers grading the same paper, and that, if the same teacher was given the same paper to grade after a period of time, his *own two* grades would frequently vary that much.

The question was raised loud and clear: if grades were going to play such an important role in determining a student's academic career, shouldn't teachers ensure that these wide variations in their grading practices be eliminated.

So educators began moving away from the 100-point scale to those scales which had fewer and larger categories. One was a three-point scale, which employed Excellent, Average or Poor as the grading criteria. Another was the familiar five-point scale— Excellent, Good, Average, Poor, Failing (or *A, B, C, D, F*). Some educators even considered using a seven-point scale.

Investigators discovered that as many as twenty distinct grading systems were being used in high schools and colleges.[6,7] One popular new method was "grading on a curve."[8] This meant that in any group of students, a certain few would get the highest and the lowest grades, while the majority of students would get the average grades. The aim of this system was to insure a fair distribution of grades. One advocate suggested that 2% of the students should qualify for an *A* grade, 23% for a *B*, 50% for a *C*, 23% for a *D*, and 2% should fail.

"Grading on a curve is ridiculous," Leroy Aimes said. "Some groups of students are bound to be brighter than others. Giving only 2 *A*'s for every 100 students, and then having to balance those 2 *A*'s with 2 *F*'s would be just as unfair."

Sandy spoke up this time. "As a matter of fact, that was one of the criticisms of the curve system. But you have to realize that this was just one of many grading systems which were being tried as a result of the Starch and Elliot findings. Nobody seemed to know what they were doing. What had been the most popular form of grading was now shown to be unreliable, so everyone was running around trying to find a better answer."

1920-1930

In the 1920's the shift away from the 0-100 scale continued;[10,11,12] but no one could seem to agree on what should replace it. More schools shifted to the five-point scale (*A, B, C, D, F*), based on percentages. Since they felt there wasn't any meaningful difference betwen 82 and 86, they could consider both marks as a *B*.

"But what about the difference between 78 and 82?" asked Ned Fusari. "That's certainly different from 82 and 86. A four-point span exists between both numbers, but with the use of letter grading, the 78 is not any better than a 70!"

Terry looked at his panel, but none of them seemed to have any answer.

"Well, your point is certainly valid," said Terry, "but at that time many people thought that those differences in percentages didn't mean much and that a five-point scale would make more sense."

"I don't think either one makes sense," Maria Rivera said.

"Well, I guess a lot of other people agreed with you, because *A, B, C, D, F* was only one of many grading systems used in an effort to answer the problem.

Those who advocated the grading curve also realized that every classroom did not contain a cross-section of the population. Many solutions were offered. Some educators thought that students in a class should be given IQ tests (IQ testing was becoming more and more popular), and based on the results, a certain number of *A's, B's, C's* and so on should be given in that classroom. For example, if all the students in the class were really brilliant, as shown on the IQ test, then they would be expected to get mostly *A's* and *B's*. If all the students in the class had low IQ's, then no one would be allowed to get *A's*; the teacher would have to give mostly *C's, D's* and *F's*.

"Hey, isn't that what we have now? The honors classes in this school get almost all *A*'s, and the slow classes aren't allowed to get *A*'s, I hear."

The class got into an argument about whether this was true and whether it was fair, but the bell rang ending the discussion.

The next morning, Terry began where he had left off.

Still another alternative popular in the 20's was to use words like "Excellent," "Good," and "Fair" instead of *A*, *B*, and *C*, but still based on the same percentages.

All these attempts were aimed at objectifying, standardizing and simplifying the grading process. One attempt at objectivity was to record descriptive behaviors about character traits or ratings of character traits. Teachers would rate students on appearance, motivation, citizenship, conduct, and so on. If these subjective judgments could be given a *separate* place in the overall evaluation of the students, then it was hoped the teachers would be less subjective when grading academic areas. But, as you might guess, very few people liked this alternative because there was even less objectivity by teachers when they had to grade areas involving their own value judgments.

However, not all the solutions were aimed at correcting the problems of percentage and letter grading by becoming more objective—using the grading curve, and so on. There was a large movement at this time to get away from the concept of grading altogether. A number of schools completely abolished formal grades.[13] Some used only verbal descriptions of the students' abilities. Others advocated pass-fail systems in which only the division between acceptable and failing work was determined. Some advocated a "mastery approach," saying that the only important factor was whether or not a student had mastered the information or the skill. Once mastered, he should be free to move on to other areas.

At this point, Gary Stovall, the fifth committee member, who hadn't spoken yet, interrupted Terry.

"What I find interesting is that we're going through the exact same process today. A lot of people are yelling that we should reform the grading system to correct its shortcomings; others are saying we should do away with grading altogether."

"Thank you, Mr. Stovall," said Terry in the voice of a serious T.V. moderator.

In the 1920's, one study compiled a list of 49 different bases for the various grading systems being used at that time.[14] There was mounting evidence that academic grades often reflected both arbitrary criteria and peculiar value systems of the individual teacher.

1930-1940

In the 1930's, the same two groups who held opposing views on grading continued to clash—one group wanting to eliminate grades, and the other wanting to keep them but make them more objective and scientific. The problem was that these two groups were extensions of two forces already popular in American education.

One force was the testing movement which had begun during the First World War and had been growing since then. Educators were placing great stress on the acquisition of knowledge and methods of measuring this learning. Advances in science and technology and measurement led to the rapid development of the standardized test. Many educators saw testing and measurement as one answer to many of education's problems, and they tried to bring testing and measurement into more and more facets of the school's operation.

The other force, the progressives in education, were interested in the growth of the total person, individual differences and individualized instruction. They admitted that testing and measurement could be helpful in education but were suspicious about its over-use. They were also worried about the relationship of testing and measurement to competition in schools. They began to ask what effect competitive testing might have on the personal life of the student. They also questioned the usefulness, in terms of the student's later role in society, of the material he was presently being tested on.

The following arguments seem representative of much of the criticism voiced at that time: [15]

1. Grades are unscientific, subjective and seldom relative to educational objectives.
2. They are misleading and focus only on one aspect of the child.
3. They promote superficial, spurious and insincere scholarship.
4. They lead to uncreative teaching.
5. They form a barrier between students and teachers.
6. Pupils perform for the grade and, as a result, show less initiative and independence.
7. Grades tend to divide students into recognizable groups, reflecting inferior and superior qualities, thus often becoming the basis for social relationships.

8. They establish a competitive system, with grades as the basis for achievement.

The proponents felt that by replacing grades with a more descriptive method of written evaluation, both parents and students would be better informed; relations between parent, student and teacher would improve; and the school would be seen more as a place of learning rather than a place that just gave grades. Critics of grading were not advocating the elimination of evaluation of the student's progress; they also did recognize the value of periodic examinations. Their aim was to change the grading system to a system of better communication, more meaningful evaluation and more learning.

On the issue of motivation, many educators felt that grading conditioned the student with less ability to accept failure and to accept himself as a failure.[16,17] At the same time, they argued that the brighter students would eventually show their excellence without the artificial stimulus of grades. The atmosphere within the school would also change considerably if, instead of competing, students were encouraged to share and help one another in the learning process.[18] They felt that this cooperative spirit would be driven out of the student, before many years passed, if the trend toward constant competition continued. They feared that the child would instead learn to cheat and become self-centered.

Others believed that the fault did not lie in the grading system, since there would always be the need for methods of comparing levels of student achievement. The major fault lay with those who misused

> the grading system; and many of these problems would
> be eliminated if teachers would establish clear objec-
> tives and marking criteria, use objective examinations
> and develop a normal distribution curve when assign-
> ing marks.[19,20,21]

"Excuse me, Terry, but this sounds like some of the arguments you told us about before," Maria Rivera said.

"Yeah," said Jerry Szymanski. "Haven't we been here before?"

"Yes, we have," Sandy Farrell answered. "The reason we're repeating ourselves is because *history* is repeating itself. The same arguments had been made nearly a quarter of a century earlier after the Starch and Elliot study. During the time in between, people were trying various alternatives, but the issues were always the same: Do you eliminate grades or do you make them more objective?"

"Terry, maybe you could eliminate reading those sections pertaining to the 40's and 50's. After all, they just repeat what came before—the same old arguments about the grades, the same old going back and forth between different systems."

"O.K., Sandy, but there are just a couple of points I would like to make to illustrate what Sandy meant by saying that the methods of grading went back and forth. We found out some information about the history of grading in the Philadelphia school system. I think this will give you a pretty good picture of what we've been talking about. I made these charts, so I'll just hang them up here for you to see." [22, 23]

THE CHANGING NATURE OF ELEMENTARY SCHOOL GRADES IN PHILADELPHIA SCHOOLS, 1913-1961

1913 A ten-point system was used with numbers defined as:

10	distinguished	*Students were given only*
9	excellent	*one number to denote*
		all-around progress. An
8	good	*X was placed beside any*
7	fair	*subject the student was*
		failing. Conduct and ef-
6	poor	*fort were graded by*
5-1	very poor	*letters.*

1922 In response to the criticisms of percentage grading and definitive point systems, there was a shift to a five-letter code (i.e., *E* for excellent) to replace the numbers. All subjects were marked.

1934 Increasing pressure for a less mechanical and more counseling-oriented grading system led to a three symbol approach with *A*—Outstanding, *B*—Satisfactory, and *C*—Needs Improvement. A check beside a subject revealed progress being made. Also, ten traits of citizenship were graded.

1940 Movement to a two-letter system—Satisfactory

and Unsatisfactory—plus trait checklist and indication of improvement in specific subjects.

1948 Addition of *O* for Outstanding work and *I* for Improvement.

1954 With pressure for more definitive grading increasing, shift to five-point system (*A, B, C, D, F*).

1961 *A* to *E* system supplemented with special performance checks made in particular skill areas, such as reading and arithmetic.

TO PRESENT The introduction of primary and middle schools has reduced pressure for grading in the first four years where a mastery approach to learning is being developed. Nevertheless, for parent review, letter grades are used to describe performance throughout the elementary system.

THE CHANGING NATURE OF SECONDARY SCHOOL GRADES IN PHILADELPHIA SCHOOLS, 1910-1955

1910 Each subject area graded independently according to a percentage system.

1920 In response to the criticisms of the 0-100% system, letter symbols, each relating to a particular set of percentage equivalents, were introduced. *Excellent* — 91%-100%; *Good* — 81%-90%; *Fair* — 71%-80%; *Passing* — 61%-70%; *Deficient* — below 61%.

1921 High schools dropped the percentages as equivalents to letter grades and retained only the five-point letter system.

1945 High schools revived an equivalent system, expanding it to six points. Thus, A — 90-100, B — 80-89, C — 75-79, D — 70-74, E — 60-69, F — below 60.

1955 A return to the five-point A to E system. Grades for behavior and work habits are included.

"I can't believe it!" Carla Heckman said. "Why should they go back and forth like that?"

"That's what I was wondering." Leroy Aimes stated. "First they have a ten-point system, then a three-point system, then a two-point system, then back to a three-point system, then a five-. Why? Where's the reason, the logic?"

"That's hard to answer," said Barry Binson. "Sometimes the changes were influenced by history. For instance, the 1934 change in the elementary schools came at a time when people were getting tired of all that measurement and were starting to pay more attention to understanding the child and helping him, rather than just labeling him.

"Many times, though, the changes were arbitrary ones. A controversy would start somewhere, for some reason, and someone would decide to solve the problem by changing the grading system to a five-point scale. Meanwhile, somewhere else, someone else decided that what their school needed was a good three-point grading system."

"If I may," Terry interrupted, "I'd just like to read this passage to conclude this section."

> Despite all the fluctuations, the trend was toward the five-point system.[24] By the end of the 1940's, approximately more than 80% of the nation's schools had some form of the five-point (A,B,C,D,F) system.[25] Again, the major reasons for this seemed to be administrative ease and a procedure which satisfied the universities to which the schools' graduates sought admission.
>
> During the 40's, the 50's and even the 60's, there was still talk about normal curves, objectivity, specifying grading criteria, behavioral objectives, student motivation, parent involvement, problems of reliability and validity, superficial descriptions, grade competition and damaged self-concepts. Yet the actual impact of all this talk on the grading systems seemed to make little difference with regard to what was actually being done. At no time did the report card show a statement of clear objectives nor were clear grading criteria established. People argued back and forth, tried new systems and tried old systems, but history kept repeating itself. No one seemed to have *the* answer.

Terry heaved a long sigh, and several students, as well as Mr. Cannon, thought he was done.

"Is that it, Terry?" Mr. Cannon asked.

"Not quite," said Terry. "We still have the 60's"

"Oh, no," said Maria. "More of the same? We must know the arguments by heart now."

"Don't worry, Maria" said Betty Stone. "Believe it or not, there were some new developments in that decade."

THE 1960's

This was the decade of student power, student demonstrations and student revolts on the campuses, as well as in the society. One of the main things that students were (and still are) demanding was a better education. On many campuses students saw grades as a major obstacle to getting a better education. Pressure from the students to eliminate grades was frequently supported by sympathetic faculty members. Some faculty members even took public stands against the grading system and refused to give grades. In some cases they gave all their students A's as a form of protest.

This pressure against grading began to show results in the late 60's. Yale University, which had clung to the numerical scale, finally abandoned it and converted to a four-point scale—Honors, High Pass, Pass, Fail, with no cumulative average computed. Many other colleges and universities shifted to three-point scales: Honors, Pass, Fail; or to two-point scales: Pass, Fail; Credit, No Credit; Satisfactory, Unsatisfactory. Some schools instituted these changes for the entire school, and some allowed students to take only some of their courses on a pass/fail basis.

Institutions experimenting with such grading systems ranged from small, secular colleges such as Florida Presbyterian, to private, ivy-league colleges, like Dartmouth and Brown, to universities the size of Michigan State and the University of Wisconsin. Other colleges and universities undertaking some form of pass/fail grading were: Columbia, Case Western

Reserve, Haverford, Connecticut College, Tufts, Lake Forest, Carleton, Grinnell, Simmons, Bowdoin, Harvard, La Salle, Princeton, Ohio State, University of Chicago, University of Washington, Washington State University, Penn State, California Institute of Technology, University of California at Berkeley, Temple University Medical College and Douglass College, to name just a few.

"How do we know this isn't just a temporary historical movement, as in the past?" Ed Hecht asked.

"Because this time it's different," Betty said. "In the past, the elementary schools and high schools went back and forth between two-point systems and five- or more point systems. But this time many colleges are adopting the new grading system.

"Why aren't the high schools changing as fast?" Cannon asked.

Gary Stovall answered. "I think it's because they are scared the colleges won't like it—they might be prejudiced against kids who apply from high schools without grades."

"Yeah," Barry Binson said. "But, funny enough, that's what all the *colleges* were scared of—that their graduates wouldn't get into graduate schools. But many of them went ahead and eliminated grades, and many graduate schools are accepting the college graduates without grades."

"What do the graduate schools use to decide which students to accept?" Debbie Richmond asked.

"Letters of recommendation, Graduate Record Exam scores and interviews," Terry said. "It seems to work out well. Kids who get high grades usually get high GRE scores, anyway, so grades don't add much."

"But, you know, from what I've been reading," Sandy Farrell said, "apparently the high schools are going to start to eliminate grades also. I think what's going to happen is that high schools are going to start doing what the colleges did. They're going to start to eliminate grades even though they may be taking a chance, hoping colleges will accept the students anyway, and then other schools will see this and start to eliminate grades also. In other words, the whole movement is going to filter down from the colleges and universities to the high schools."

"How do you know?" Barry Binson asked. "If we were alive in the 20's when there was a shift away from percentage grading, we might have predicted that the death of grades was around the corner. But look what happened. After a while, there was a shift back to more complicated grading systems."

"Yes, but it's different today," Sandy answered. "As I said, it's the colleges that have started the trend this time. Remember when that other committee gave its report on the history of the changing high school curriculum? They showed us how Harvard's and Yale's entrance requirements became the standard high school curriculum. Well, the same thing could happen here. The colleges will pave the way. We read now of many high schools that have eliminated grading in their 9th and 10th grades, and several which have abolished grading altogether. I tell you, the trend has already started."

"Listen, I'm sorry to have to break in here." It was Mr. Cannon. He had risen from the desk in the back of the room and walked down the aisle by the windows, until he was standing near Terry's committee in front.

"This is really interesting and I'd like to keep it going, but we've got several other committees' reports to hear, and if we want to finish before Thanksgiving, we're going to have to move on. You've certainly given us a whole lot to think about. I wonder whether anyone on your committee would like to sum up or maybe talk a little about what you got out of this project—what you learned from it."

The panel looked back and forth at each other for a minute, and then, as if some unspoken consensus had been reached, Sandy Farrell indicated she would be the one.

"Well, we talked a bit about this ourselves, and I think this was really an eye-opening research project for us. Speaking for myself, I realize how little intelligent educational basis there is for our grading system. Sure, it's convenient for schools. They can use grades to decide who gets scholarships, to select the valedictorian, to determine who gets put on academic probation, to pick those who can join the honor society, and so on. And it certainly is a convenient way for colleges to select candidates, even if they don't have the slightest idea what a student's grades mean.

"But, when you look back over the history of grades, you can't help thinking how ludicrous it all is. Here we've been accepting grades for eleven years as if they were as natural as the rain. We assumed that grading came with Adam and would be here until doomsday. We just accepted the whole system, believing that since it existed, there must be a good reason for it.

"Well, I learned from this report that there *are* reasons, historical reasons, why grading exists. But I also learned from history that there are no *good* reasons— no sound educational ones, anyway—why they should continue to exist."

Walter Cannon's class *did* complete their reports before Thanksgiving. Mr. Cannon had to smile with slight uneasiness as he entered *A*'s in his role book next to the names of Terry Hansen, Betty Stone, Barry Binson, Gary Stovall and Sandy Farrell.

5 | *The Alumnus and the Grading Game*[1]

It was the week after Thanksgiving.

The bell rang, noting the end of second period, but at least six minutes before, the students had started to gather together their notebooks and pens and other student paraphernelia, and pile them up in one corner of their desks for a quick getaway. One girl, who had a boyfriend to meet by the corner of the second floor locker room, was through the door before the echo of the bell had died away.

"What's the assembly today?" Jim Rogers asked his friend Gary.

"I don't know. Hey, Greg, what's on for the assembly?" Greg Sanford usually knew that kind of thing.

"Some guy who graduated from Mapleton High and made out real big at Berkeley," Greg answered.

"You mean he was in on that Free Speech Movement and all that radical stuff they had out there?" Jim questioned.

"Not *this* guy," Greg said. "This one is a brain. He knocked off the top grade point average, made Phi Beta Kappa, and got offered jobs and scholarships from every big company and graduate school in the country. At least, that's what Mr. Harper said."

"Do you want to try and cut it?" Gary asked his two friends.

"Ah, it's not worth the risk," Greg said. "I'm going to bring a magazine to kill the time. The lights will be on. They usually are for a speech."

"Don't bring *Playboy*. I got detention after the last assembly when I pulled one out. I waited til the 200th slide of Yosemite, and then couldn't take any more," Jim groaned.

The friends went their separate ways to dump books into lockers and to pick up magazines to fortify themselves against the assembly.

The auditorium was noisy. All the doors were open, and the students slowly and raucously drifted toward their assigned seats. Greg could see the speaker on the podium. He was complete with glasses, neat hair and what looked like a watch fob.

The teachers were standing in the aisles, roll books open, checking attendance. They knew that this was hardly a pep rally so there would be many cuts.

Something confused Greg. Cliff Harper, easily Mapleton High's most popular science teacher and probably *the* best-liked teacher in the whole school, was up on the platform, too. Apparently Harper was going to introduce the speaker, which meant that the brain up there with the watch fob might have something interesting to say. When Harper had a friend who was an ex-student, that friend always had some recommendation other than high grades.

When all the students were seated, Mr. Cunningham gave the signal, and the student body rose to dutifully sing "The Star-Spangled Banner." Then the principal made a few announcements: a foreign exchange student was coming so would someone please volunteer a house; the Red Cross drive would start Monday; and the band would be wearing their new uniforms at the annual Christmas concert—be sure to invite your parents. "And now it is my pleasure to call on Mr. Harper to introduce our speaker for the morning."

As Mr. Harper rose and walked to the lecturn, with one hand in his pocket, there was applause and many whistles from the 10th grade homerooms laden with students in Mr. Harper's biology sections.

"Students, faculty and guests. It is a rare privilege and a personal honor to introduce today's speaker to you. His name is Robert MacIntyre, a graduate of the class of 1964 here at Mapleton High. Some of you had brothers or sisters who were classmates of Bob Mac-Intyre's, but I doubt they would have predicted that he would someday be invited to speak at an assembly here at Mapleton High.

"I had Bob in a bio class back when he was a sophomore, and I hope he won't mind my saying that he didn't, at *that* time, know one end of a frog from another. Well, once he got out under the California sun, not only did he learn which end of a frog was up, but Robert MacIntyre graduated from Berkeley last year with the highest grade-point average in the College of

Letters and Science, which is no mean trick, as some of you can imagine."

The students in the audience seemed singularly unimpressed. Some had already started reaching for magazines or textbooks to complete some of their homework.

"It's a real pleasure to introduce an alumnus of Mapleton High who is going to speak on the subject of 'High School as a Preparation for College.' May I present Robert MacIntyre."

While Mr. Harper was making his way back to his seat, the sound of thin applause was barely audible. He shook hands with Bob, who was striding to the lectern. Bob spent just a little too long getting his notes in order, and the students began to fidget.

"Thank you, Mr. Harper," he began. His hands gripped the lectern and moved up the slanting part in rhythm with his words. "You were correct in noting that I was graduated from the University of California, Berkeley, with the highest grade-point average in the College of Letters and Science."

Someone in the fifth row whispered, "big deal," and the students around him laughed nervously, hoping their homeroom teacher would not blame them for the remark.

"This was probably the reason I was asked to come to Mapleton High to speak on the topic: 'High School as a Preparation for College.'

"Yes, I *did* achieve a remarkable record, but the message that I would like to leave with you today, and probably one of the most important things I learned in college, is that *my single-minded pursuit of high grades has simply not been worth it.*"

Some students, amazed by what they thought they had just heard, stopped flipping through their magazines.

"The grade-point game kept me from the real goal of education: the development of myself as a person. I have come to believe that the traditional system of grading should be eliminated and replaced by one of the alternatives, like pass/fail grading which so many colleges have begun to implement.

"I spent four years in college before I realized that grades are a major obstacle to teaching and to learning. My own experience in secondary school, right here at Mapleton High, should have shown me the pitfalls of traditional grading, but the system was working to my advantage, I thought, so I wasn't about to question the damage it was also doing. My friends and I—some of them maybe your brothers or sisters, as Mr. Harper said —learned to play the grade-point game with consummate skill. We were preparing for college, and we were told, time and again, that we had to follow the rules in high school so we would be admitted to the ivy leagues.

"Let me ask you: How many times have you heard, 'If you want to get into college, you'll have to work harder than that'? Or, 'You won't get away with *that* in college'? Or what about, 'In college, they'll expect you to do it this way'? Judging from your reaction, I can see these aren't unfamiliar statements.

"And the sad thing is, most of us never questioned the rules. Now that I look back upon both high school and college, I view the whole grading system as unfortunate. My major objection to the form of grading used while I was in school is that the grades usually became the sought-after goal rather than merely symbolizing what had been learned. In most of my courses, my classmates and I were concerned not with how much we were going to learn, but with how much knowledge we had to digest in order to get a high grade.

"Does anyone doubt this? If you do, think about that infamous word 'Wad-ja-get . . . ?' Wad-ja-get? It bounces up and down the halls of Mapleton High hundreds of times a day. When you ask a friend, at the end of a semester, 'Wad-ja-get?', do you expect him to evaluate what he got out of the content of the course? Do you expect an answer in words or sentences or paragraphs even? No, you expect to hear one single letter of the alphabet—*A* or *B* or *C* or *D* or *F,* and perhaps a plus or minus after it. When your parents ask you, 'How are you doing in school?', who among you does not know how to translate that question?

"I had several sincere, dedicated and competent teachers when I was at Mapleton High; and many of them are still here. But all their efforts were undermined because we, their students, were working for *grades* rather than for what we could *learn* from them.

"Whenever a major exam was imminent, we began to compute exactly how much we had to know in order to

get the grade we wanted or needed. If one hour's studying was enough, one hour it was. If an allnighter was
required, so be it. If a teacher assigned a book, but
said we wouldn't be tested on it, he may as well have
never mentioned the book, because *we* sure weren't
going to read it. If an assignment were not going to be
checked or graded, that assignment was less important
to us than one which was going to be graded.

"When we asked a teacher, 'Does this count?', we were
asking whether the work would be graded; and if the
answer were 'no,' that teacher would be lucky if half
the class did the work, and even luckier if half of those
did a decent job on it.

One of my friends summarized his philosophy: we
wanted 'the best possible grade for the least possible
amount of work.' When he said this to me back in high
school . . . I remember just where it was: near the water
fountain on the third floor near Miss Stokley's room.
There never was enough pressure in that water fountain
to get a good drink. I wonder whether they've fixed it
yet."

The kids in Miss Stokley's homeroom whistled loudly.

"Well, anyway, when my friend said this to me, I pretended to be shocked by such an outlook, for I was convinced that grades were good and that I was good because of all the *A*'s I had. But now, in retrospect, I can
see that I was working within the same framework as
my friend. As did many others, I gauged my efforts on
the requirements each teacher set up for the magical *A*.

Each teacher posed a separate challenge. We would observe his tastes and preferences and then cater to them.

"I learned to jump when a teacher told me to. I learned to set my margins just where I was told to set them, and I always put in the proper number of footnotes to satisfy them. I quickly sized them up and fed them just what they wanted."

This last statement was greeted with murmurs of recognition from many of the students and frowns on several teachers' faces.

"I became a hustler. If a teacher liked Toynbee, I gave him some Toynbee on every exam. If he didn't like beat poetry, then I pretended I didn't either. If he rewarded creativity, then I was creative and gave him the kind of creativity I knew he was buying.

"And it worked; I got my *A*'s. When I got my blue-books back, I'd see that the teacher had written 'good point or some other similar phrase in the margin. When I read the paragraph to see what 'good point' I had made, I recognized that this comment referred to the teacher's own words or ideas which I had memorized from my notes and skillfully included in the test. Yes, I got my *A*'s, and I got my scholarships. But when I think of all those years, I also realize what I *lost* in the process.

"But in high school, most of us were too young or too naive to be consciously cynical about what we were doing. We had mastered the rules without realizing the destructive game we were playing. Good grades were like games won out on the ball field, and points earned in

American history were almost the same as those scored in a basketball game. The idea of competition was exalted as a good thing, both in studies and in sports. My guess is that this hasn't changed much in the four years since I left Mapleton High. It's still dog-eat-dog."

This time MacIntyre was interrupted by applause. He went on for several minutes, developing his analogy between sports and grades. Then he threw it into the audience's lap.

"Yes, they put me out on the academic playing field and told me to compete, so I competed. Just like *every student in this auditorium* is competing with every other student. That's right. Look around you. Take a look at your competition."

The students stirred uneasily, not knowing quite how to react. MacIntyre pursued his point.

"Look around you. There they are—your enemies. Don't laugh; think about it. *Your enemies.*"

He paused, hoping what he had just said would sink in and cause each student to think about what he was doing and what the results were going to be.

"There are several kinds of competition. One kind is when people *choose* to compete, according to standards they themselves have set and regard as important. I think there's a lot to be said for this kind of competition. Theoretically, everyone can be a winner.

"Another kind of competition is when people are *forced* to compete against one another, according to standards that are *imposed* upon them by others. With this kind of competition, the kind we find in schools, there must be a loser for every winner. So you see, I wasn't kidding before. You are each one another's enemy. For every winner out there, there's also a loser. Am I right?"

There was a stony silence.

"You *know* I'm right. In fact, you have probably already labelled yourself 'winner,' 'loser,' or 'in between.' If you have decided that you're a winner, then you're probably feeling a bit complacent and smug right now. But if you consider yourself a loser, you're probably annoyed and angry with me for reminding you of what your teachers have been telling you for years. Well, I've got news for you. *You are all losers!* That's right. Whether you have high grades or low grades, you're all losers because you've all been cheated out of a decent education.

"The innate curiosity you all once had, which led you to learn to walk and to speak, which led you to learn to interact with others—that inner drive for new knowledge has almost been evaporated by an educational system based on grades. Knowledge, rather than being the goal of an exciting search, has turned into discrete packets of information to be greedily acquired and then unwrapped and displayed on examination papers, and then forgotten. Despite occasional orations on the real aims of education and the fulfilling aspects of learning, the difference between what is preached to us and what is practiced on us never seems to bother anyone enough to change the over-emphasis on grades.

"So, high grades or low, we're all losers because we've

been deprived of a real education. But we're all losers in another, more profound way. A minute ago I became somewhat dramatic when I referred to you as either winners or losers. I'm sorry if I made some people uncomfortable, but I wanted you to *feel* what I was saying, the point I was making, the point that *grades become inextricably tied to a person's sense of his own worth.*

"I believe this is one of the most harmful aspects of grading. Society—our parents, our teachers, and eventually we ourselves—stresses the importance of grades so much that we come to feel that we are as good or as bad as our grades indicate. You people with high grades have been led to believe that you're somehow better than the rest. You people with low grades have been made to feel, year in and year out, that you're not as good as the others, that you just don't have what it takes. And I guess you people with average grades come to view yourselves as pretty average people—jealous that you're not up there with the best of them, but glad you're not down there with the others.

"I've often used an analogy which some people say is a bit exaggerated, but I don't think so. I think it's so true that it makes me want to cry. Imagine, for a moment, a family: father, mother and three children. At the end of each year, the parents award grades to the children which represent their overall growth during the year. Just imagine what the reaction would be when the mother said, 'Sherrie, this wasn't a very good year for you; we're giving you a *D*.' 'Jerry, you've improved this year—*C* plus.' 'And, Estelle, I hope you'll serve as an example to your brother and sister—*A* minus.' Can you picture how harmful this would be; how the child would be forced to label himself; how he would be set against his brother and his sister; how such unfavorable grades would destroy the child's desire to improve; how this competitive evaluation would create hostility toward the parents; how the child would be forced to become subservient to the parents and adopt all the parents' values so he could attain or maintain the love and affection that go with high grades?

"So help me, this is *exactly* what we do in schools. We don't want to, but we do. We don't give just one grade, we give several, even though we know that the correlation between grades in different subjects is so high that we might as well give one grade. We force students to label themselves. We create hostility between students and teachers and between students and students. And we force the student to prostitute himself in order to get those grades.

"'We destroy the love of learning in children by encouraging them and compelling them to work for petty and contemptible rewards—gold stars, or papers marked 100 and tacked to the wall, or *A*'s on report cards, or honor rolls, or dean's lists, or **Phi Beta Kappa** keys—in short, for the ignoble satisfaction of feeling that they are better than someone else.'²

"The fact is, whether a person gets high grades or low ones or even average ones has *nothing* to do with whether or not he is a good, a courageous, a loving, a beautiful or a worthy person. For too long now, you've been indoctrinated to believe that grades represent the measure of a person's value. But one day the fallacy of this premise will hit you. And if it hits you as it hit me, then it's going to hit hard.

"Some of you, perhaps, may be wondering what made me change from the grade-grubbing student I have been describing to one who is now advocating the elimination of traditional grading.

"The shift occurred gradually, I suppose, yet in my mind I see one evening in the spring of last year as being the real turning point. I was sitting in my apartment in Berkeley thinking about what I was going to do the following year. I had scholarship offers from at least a dozen graduate schools, in addition to very promising job offers from several large corporations. I sat there with all the letters and information in front of me and felt paralyzed. They were offering me lots of money, promising careers, prestigeous academic institutions to attend—everything I had ever wanted, everything I had been working for—yet I couldn't choose.

"In the past I had always taken the best opportunity that came along. I went to Berkeley when I was graduated from high school because they offered me the biggest scholarship. I majored in history because I had always gotten my best grades in that subject, and because I had found history the easiest subject to do well in. I even played soccer in high school because the gym teacher needed more men, and he said I could make the team. Yet, here I was, having to choose from among *many* excellent alternatives, and I found myself immobilized.

"I've dashed off more 30-page term papers than I care to remember, and I have breezed through all the multiple choice tests I was given; but here I was, confronted with one of the biggest choices in my life, and I couldn't make a decision.

"Then it gradually dawned on me: I had no idea what I *really* wanted to do with my life. I could go to grad school and be pretty certain of more success, more honors and more rewards. But honors and rewards suddenly lost their meaning for me because I began to see the pattern by which I had been living my whole life.

"When I was a child, my parents patted me on the head for doing some things, but withdrew their rewards when I did other things. So I began to conform to *their* values and expectations because those pats on the head were pretty important to me. When I got to school, the teachers hit me with the importance of getting good grades. They made grades seem so important that I soon believed them. But in order to get good grades, I had to conform to *their* values and expectations, which I did. So again, I got more pats on the head. And the subjects in which I got the most pats on the head were the subjects I decided I liked the most.

"I kept striving for high marks, never questioning

why and for whom, never realizing what was happening until that night last spring when I had to make a choice and realized that, somewhere along the line, I had never developed *my own* values, *my own* likes and dislikes, *my own* passions and causes. That's why I couldn't decide. Because I had been so busy getting grades that I didn't take the time to discover who I was and what I wanted to do with my life. While thousands of students all around me at Berkeley were becoming involved and taking sides in the great social issues of the day, I was conforming to the pressures of a grading system which was standing in the way of my real education."

MacIntyre took his hands off the lectern and came around to the side of it, as though he wanted to get closer to the students. Then he said, "And my hunch is that there are hundreds of you in this auditorium who, even though a few years younger than I, are doing just as I did.

"I want to tell you that I am convinced that my life is less beautiful because I played that grading game. I am convinced that schools will never *really* teach if they continue to rely on grades. I have made a serious mistake and have missed what learning is all about. If I had my school life to do over again, I would never have tried to collect all those *A*'s. They have gotten between me and life; and I say to you, life is more important, more interesting and more challenging than any number of *A*'s, if they were piled from here to the moon."

He moved back behind the lectern again. "There is

still time for all of you. There is still time to stop con-
centrating on marks and to start focusing on *learning*.
There is still time to develop *your own* learning goals and
values and to then pursue those instead of grades. There
is still time to influence your institution to reconsider its
grading system. There is still time to get rid of that word
'Wad-ja-get?' which has come to characterize our education.

"If you were to ask me today, 'Wad-ja-get?', I would
have to honestly answer, 'I got all *A*'s, and not one of
them was worth it. Not one of them.' "

With that, Robert MacIntyre, class of 1964, Mapleton
High School, sat down. The applause came slowly, but
then started to swell, and it grew and grew. Some students started to stand while they were clapping, and soon
others stood. MacIntyre received the first standing ova-
tion anyone could ever remember in Mapleton High's
auditorium.

Finally, Mr. Cunningham walked to the front of the
platform. "Thank you very much, Mr. MacIntyre.
We're always glad when our alumni get a chance to
come back and see us at Mapleton High. And thank
you, Mr. Harper, for arranging for us to hear Mr.
MacIntyre's message. Will you now please file out of
the auditorium in the usual order. The bell for fourth
period will ring five minutes later than usual. Thank
you."

6 | *Mr. Cannon's Class Begins a Project*

MR. MACINTYRE'S SPEECH had a dramatic effect on the climate at Mapleton High. He had touched upon one of the most important aspects in the daily operation of any school. Reverberations could be heard up and down the halls. Before long, parents were calling Mr. Cunningham to criticize him and the school for allowing this "campus radical" to come and undermine their sons' and daughters' motivation and respect for education. Mr. Cunningham had all he could do to assure his callers that reports concerning this "Phi Beta Kappa student's thought-provoking address" had been "highly exaggerated."

The day after the speech, students in many classrooms were discussing the pros and cons of what MacIntyre had said. They were generally in agreement that grading was, in fact, a "game" which often interfered with their education. They felt they were, indeed, "selling themselves" to earn high grades. However, most students were reluctant to consider seriously the abandoning of grades. Some frankly said they could not see themselves really working without grades; others saw no better alternatives; and others feared that without grades they would not be accepted into good colleges.

The faculty was also divided on the issue. Some, like Crewson of the History Department, were outraged by MacIntyre's remarks and demanded that, in the future, all speeches be screened by Mr. Cunningham to avoid "irresponsible and disrespectful" content. Other teachers, both those who agreed with the alumnus' views and those who disagreed, felt that the speech interested the students and made them think; and this was justification enough.

"They must have been interested," stated Burkhardt, the assistant principal. "I didn't have to throw one kid out during the assembly."

In Cannon's history class, the discussion was the liveliest of all. Since they had been examining the grading issue for almost a month, they were delighted with MacIntyre's choice of subject. While most of the other classes were more or less divided on the issue of grading, Cannon's class was much closer to a consensus. As Carla Heckman put it, "Our study of the history of grading showed us that education once took place without grades. Since grading was introduced over 50 years ago, people have been aware of its shortcomings. Our present grading system has never been justified; it's never been proven that it makes the best sense. But MacIntyre said it better than any of us could, by showing us what grading does to our own education and how it perverts learning into a 'grading game.' If you want my opinion, we once got along fine without grades, and we'd do better now without them."

Most of the students in the class seemed to agree with this line of thinking. Each new comment pointed out another drawback of grading. As one thought led to another, there was that special kind of group dynamic which often occurs when people are simultaneously moved by the power of a new idea, or at least an idea which is new to them.

Mary Ellen Wheeler asked, "If you do away with grades, what are you going to put in their place?" But no one seemed to pick up on her point.

After a while, Cannon pointed out to the class that the same points were being repeated and that the discussion seemed to be losing its momentum.

"Mr. Cannon's right," Terry Hansen said. "Personally, I'm tired of talking about grades. I've talked about grades as long as I've been in school, and that seems like a long time. We've talked about grades in this class before. We've talked about the history of grading. The guy in the assembly talked about grades. And here we are again, talking about grades. But that's all we do around here: *Talk*.

"I'd like to stop *talking* about grades and start *doing* something for a change. Most of us seem to be in agreement here, and I know that a lot of other kids agree with what MacIntyre said. If this class is so dead-set against grades, then why don't we try to do something to change the grading system in this school?"

All eyes turned toward Mr. Cannon.

"Why are you looking at me?" he asked.

"Well, can we?" Jerry Szymanski inquired.

"Can you what?"

"Can we do something about grades in this school?"

Cannon smiled. "I think I hear two different questions there, Jerry. One is can you, that is, will I *allow* you to spend class time working on such a project? The answer to that is easy. Yes, if enough of you want to do it. The other question I hear is whether you will accomplish anything through your efforts. That is, can you succeed in making any changes in the grading system, or will you be wasting your time? The answer to that one is a lot harder. All I know is this: changing the system won't be easy."

The class sat thoughtfully for a while.

"You mean you'd actually let us spend class time on this?" Gail Kaufman asked.

"Sure," Cannon said. "We history teachers are supposed to teach you about politics, for one thing. I have a hunch if you undertake this project, you're going to learn a lot about politics. We're also supposed to teach you to be 'responsible citizens.' Well, I suspect we'll all learn a bit about what that entails, too."

Maria Rivera had an idea. "Hey, our class is assigned one afternoon in March to put on an assembly for the school. Maybe we can use that assembly time to report to the school the results of our project."

"That's fine with me," Cannon replied. "The question is whether you want to."

After another fifteen minutes of discussion and after

several unsuccessful attempts by some students to rail-road the class into a unanimous decision, the class was still divided on the question. Three of the twenty-eight students favored the present grading system. Four others were undecided about their stand on grading and did not care to pursue the topic further. Another four were against grading but did not care strongly enough about the issue to spend more class time on it. Three members were undecided but wanted to undertake the class project anyway. Twelve members were against grading and wanted to make an effort to change the school's grading system. Two students were absent. Most of the fifteen who wanted to undertake the project were quite enthusiastic about the idea, and emotions flared up on both sides.

"What's the matter with you? Don't you *care* about your education?"

"I think it will be a total waste of time. You're not going to change anything, no matter what you do or say."

"How do you know until you try?"

"Let's take a vote."

"You just want to get rid of grades so you don't have to work."

"Didn't you learn *anything* from the history of grading?"

"Here's our chance to finally do something, instead of just talking all the time."

"Let's take a vote."

Cannon was pleased with the enthusiasm shown in

the discussion but bothered by the process.

"You know," he interrupted, "it amazes me how easily democracy is abused. I don't mean just in this class. I see it outside all the time. Here, I see you're getting ready to take a vote. Each side has tried to talk the other side out of its position. Now that the lines have hardened, you're getting frustrated and want to get the voting over with. You people in favor of the grading project clearly have the majority. I can see your getting the vote in favor of your stand and then gloating because the whole class is going to have to do the project. You wouldn't really care that one-third of the group was against the idea. But later you'd wonder why you weren't getting anywhere. And as for you people against the project, I don't know why *you're* looking so smug. If you were in the majority, you'd probably have done the same thing they were ready to do to you.

"Most people today see democracy as: debate, vote, and winner take all. But doesn't the majority have a responsibility to the minority? I think it does. Why does every student in this class have to be doing the same thing, even when there is no need for sameness, as in this case?

"Now, how many people want to work on the grading project? Okay, you fifteen are the grading committee. Now, how many of you want to work on the play? Fine. You eleven are the play group. How's that? Is anybody unhappy? As long as we're individualizing here, there's no reason why we can't have more than two groups, is there . . . ? No takers . . .? OK, then, two projects it is. Now, doesn't that brand of democracy make more sense?"

The class filed out slowly, stinging a bit from their teacher's criticism of their process. But they were happy with the final results and were looking forward to the adventure ahead.

As Maria Rivera left the room, she called back to Cannon, "Hey, Mr. Cannon, where do *you* stand on this issue of grading? How are you going to grade us on our grading project?"

7 | The Teacher's Dilemma over Grading

WALTER CANNON had been procrastinating for almost a hour, fixing a doornob in the bathroom; but at 8:30 he finally seated himself in his study with the stack of twenty-five history tests from his ninth grade class.

At an in-service meeting two years before, the Assistant Superintendent in Charge of Curriculum and Instruction had told the faculty what research had concluded about the grading of papers.[1] First of all, the teachers had been told, cover up the names of the students or use code numbers so that partiality toward or against particular students will not affect your grading. Then take question number one and grade it on each paper. When you've completed number one, grade number two on each paper, and so on, until all the questions are completed. Then simply tally the numbers, uncover the students' names and enter the grades in the book.

Cannon appreciated the suggestion at the time but never seemed to get around to utilizing the recommended method. Perhaps to assuage some of his guilt, he had taken an informal survey among the faculty three months after the Assistant Superintendent's speech. As far as he could determine, Russ Collins was about the only teacher who actually graded papers that way.

"I'd be bored to death if I had to read answers to the same question twenty or thirty times in a row," Elizabeth Gewirtz said. "I tried it once, and after the fifth paper all the answers began sounding exactly the same."

"I make every effort to grade objectively," Grace Merrill replied. "I just don't see the need to do my grading the way he suggested."

"If I graded like that," Jerry Garrison told Cannon, "I'd find it much harder to take individual differences into account."

So much for the research Walter Cannon thought, as he heaved a sigh of resignation, picked up Eddie Sawyer's exam paper and began to read it.

The first three papers went easily—an *A,* a *B,* and a *C+.* The grades seemed to fit the papers perfectly. When he got to Andrea Goodman's paper, he had trouble deciding between a *B* and a *B+*; but since Andrea was generally a good student, he gave her the benefit of the doubt. The next paper was an obvious *C* and caused no problem; but the next one was tricky—it was Donald Smith's.

Donald was one of those students who just didn't work. Cannon often thought that if Donald were in a sinking lifeboat, he'd barely have the motivation to bail. Cannon had been having such a hard time getting Donald to work that he had spoken to Mrs. Schmidt Donald's guidance counselor.

Mrs. Schmidt looked over the boy's records. "Donald

is a typical case," she said. "We get the same kind of reports on him every year. As you see here, his I.Q. is average, and he reads at his proper grade level, but he just doesn't work. Oh, occasionally he gets interested in something, but the spark never lasts."

As Cannon began reading the paper, he was pleasantly surprised. Donald was waxing eloquently about Caesar's military conquests and campaigns. He included ideas and facts which Cannon had brought up in class; he cited an anecdote from the textbook; and he even had some information which was unfamiliar to Cannon.

Cannon recalled that neither he nor Donald had left the room during the test, and he also knew that Donald was not taking Latin, which would have accounted for the additional information about Caesar. There could be no other explanation—Donald Smith had recently done some outside reading. The information he'd included could not possibly have been remembered from a book report from previous years.

Cannon was practically elated as he turned the page and found more of the same. It was too good to be true. This was one of those occasional times to which Mrs. Schmidt had referred that Donald was interested in school work. Three pages of Julius Caesar and Donald was still going strong. But when Cannon turned to page four and saw more of the same, a sense of impending gloom slowly began to settle over him.

Donald had written his *whole* test on this one question, but the test called for *three* essays. No one else had made that mistake. Had Donald misunderstood? Or had he not studied the other areas and was trying to bluff his way through on the strength of this one essay? Cannon bristled a little at the thought that maybe Donald was trying to con him. Statistically, Donald deserved an *A* for the first question and an *F* for each of the two others —an overall grade of *D*+. But suppose it was an honest mistake? This was the first time Donald showed any interest or effort. To give him a *D*+ would be criminal. He definitely deserved a make-up test, in this case, even though it would mean making up some new questions for Donald to answer.

Then the thought occurred to Cannon: What if Donald had purposely put all his eggs in Caesar's basket, either because that was all he had studied or because that was all he felt like writing about? In any event this paper still showed the results of more work than he'd done all semester, and was still an important learning experience for Donald. Giving him a *D*+ would probably kill any spark of motivation Donald had in him. No, Donald did not deserve a *D*+. He didn't even deserve a *C,* because a C connotes fair work, and Donald's work was better than fair. He didn't even deserve a *B,* because a *B* means good, and Donald's work was better than that. Donald deserved an *A,* because the essay itself was excellent. Cannon also wanted to give Donald an *A* because the grade might do much to encourage him to continue to improve his efforts.

But would that be fair to the other students? What

about Gary Mortimer's *B* paper? Gary had written three essays, as the test had directed, and had apparently done much more work than Donald. Although his paper was not outstanding, it clearly showed a lot of preparation and knowledge. At the time he marked it, Cannon had felt very comfortable putting a *B* on the front page. But now, didn't Gary deserve at least as much as Donald? The problem was getting complicated. Cannon was beginning to realize its ramifications.

If we give the students with less ability or less motivation low grades, then they are going to be discouraged and become less motivated. Thus, they will appear to be less able, so they will continue to get low grades, and so on. But if we grade students according to effort, then to the extent that effort plays a part in the grade, the grade is no longer an indication of ability, and begins to lose its meaning.

Cannon put Donald's paper aside, planning to get back to it later, and went into the kitchen for a beer.

Four papers and another beer later, Cannon burst out laughing and Joyce, his wife, came from the next room to find out what was so funny.

"These girls have got to be kidding," he said. "I asked them to explain why the Greeks won the Trojan war, and they both wrote, as part of their essays, 'because the Greeks bashed in the gates of Troy with a big wooden horse.' "

"Well, that is kind of funny," his wife said, "but I'm not sure I get the whole joke. You seem to think it's pretty amazing."

"Don't you see, Joyce? They were copying from each other. No two people could come up with that same wrong answer by coincidence."

"I don't know. Out of a class of twenty-five or thirty, it's possible."

"But these two sit next to each other." He smiled as though he'd won his point.

"Well, that still doesn't prove anything. Maybe they sit next to each other because they're friends, and if they're friends, maybe they study together, and if they study together, maybe they got confused about the same point together. . . ."

"Oh, Joyce, you just don't understand. Go back to your Sears catalogue," he said half jokingly.

Joyce shrugged and headed back to the living room. As she was leaving the room, she remarked, "I thought you once told me the kids in your classes don't cheat."

Her slippered feet could be heard padding down the hall.

Cannon was upset. He'd gotten only nine papers marked in almost two hours. Donald Smith's was still on the side, without a grade. And now his wife made him doubt whether he was justified in putting an *F* on each of the two girls' papers. Perhaps they *had* studied together. Probably not, but how could he be sure? He hadn't noticed them looking at each other's papers or passing notes. But then again, he couldn't see everything that went on. He pictured the accusation scene when he returned the papers. The thought of what the girls would think of him if he were wrong made him redden behind the ears. If these girls *had* cheated, he wondered, how many others might have also?

Sixteen papers were left in the unfinished pile. He put the two girls' papers on top of Donald Smith's and got up to take a break, He headed toward the living room.

"Boy, do I hate grading papers," he told Joyce.

"That sounds familiar." She looked up from her catalogue and smiled.

Cannon sat down on the newly-upholstered couch and sulked.

"Why must I be a teacher and a grader at the same time? It's like being a parent and an executioner. Or a prosecutor and a judge. Or a preacher and a pimp.² The roles just don't go together. How can they trust me to help them while they know I'm also responsible for judging them?"³

"Why do you *have to* grade them?" Joyce asked. "Why don't you hand them back with only half of the papers graded and tell the class you'll grade the other half on the next test?"

"Ha. I can just see myself doing that. They'd never go for it. They'd feel cheated somehow. If there's no grade given, then the work doesn't seem worth doing, they think. I don't blame them; I was the same way myself."

"That sure sounds like a great educational system," Joyce remarked.

"I don't know why I feel so down now," he said. "School's been pretty good this week, and some of my classes were really lively today."

Joyce knew about the class' reports on the history of grading, but now her husband brought her up to date about the latest developments in the school—the alumnus' speech, the school-wide controversy it engendered, and his class' discussion and decision to try to change the school's grading system.

"Then, as they were leaving class, Maria Rivera asked me what my position on the grading issue was. I had kept pretty much out of the discussion except for clarifying points and keeping it moving along. The way she put it was how did I plan on grading them on their grading projects? I think I've been mulling that over all afternoon. And then these papers . . ."

"Well, what *do* you think about grades, Walt?"

"I'm not sure. I've never really liked them but always assumed they were a fact of life and served their purpose. But my class' report on the history of grades made me wonder. Apparently, a lot of colleges are starting to do away with grades now, so who knows? Maybe they're not needed after all. I do know that *I'd* be a lot happier if I didn't have to give grades. I think I could actually almost look forward to reading these papers if I didn't have to grade them. I enjoy writing comments on the papers, but I always have to worry whether or not my comments are consistent with the grade, and that takes the fun out of it.

"For example, I originally wrote two comments on one particular paper tonight. One comment praised an original idea, and the other disagreed with something the student said. I forget what it was, but I asked him to consider the other side of the question which he left out of his answer. OK, that's all I really wanted to say to him; I was pleased with my comments. But then I had to grade him. In respect to the other kids' work and my expectations and all that, I thought he deserved a B-, so that's what I gave him.

"But then I realized that this kid usually gets *B+* or *A-*, so when he read my comments, he would say to himself, 'why not a *B+* or an *A-*?' So I had to go back over the paper and find places to make some more comments, in order to justify clearly the B-. The whole process of grading papers becomes a bore. I even find myself making up tests that will be easy to grade, rather than creating more interesting questions which would be harder to grade."

"*I* sure wish you didn't have to grade so many papers. I think you're a whole lot more fun to be with than this Sears catalogue."

Cannon kissed his wife, stretched out on the couch and put his head on her lap.

"Really, honey, why can't your students read and evaluate each other's papers sometimes? They could learn a lot from doing it. Why do *you* have to read each one?"

"You're right. That would be a great idea, but as

long as there's grading, it's just out of the question. Grades are too important to allow their peers to give them grades. They want me to grade them because I'll be 'fair' and 'objective.' Now I suppose I don't have to grade everything and they could evaluate each other when I don't grade them, but the trouble with that is, if you sometimes *don't* grade, the kids regard the non-graded assignments as relatively unimportant. When they ask, 'Does this count?' they are asking whether or not it will be graded. MacIntyre said something about that, and it's true. Important assignments are graded; unimportant assignments are not graded. The whole system stinks, if you ask me. But I'm damned if I know how to change it."

"What about that girl's question? Have you decided what you're going to do about grading their project on grading?"

Cannon was a long time in replying.

"I don't know. I'd like not to grade them at all, but then I'd be worried they'd consider it an unimportant unit. And some kids might not work on it. They're enthusiastic now, but who knows how long that will last? On the other hand, the more down I get on grades, the more uncomfortable I am about doing the same old thing. A lot of the kids' arguments today in class were pretty sound. I was worried they were going to turn to me and ask me not to give them grades in our class. Fortunately, they decided to tackle the problem school-wide. But it won't be long before it comes back home. I'd better give this a lot more thought, so I'll be ready. Anyway, let's sleep on it tonight."

The next morning, driving to school, Cannon was thinking about Donald Smith's and the two girls' papers. What *did* Donald deserve? And how should he approach the girls to find out whether or not they *had* cheated?

He wondered about cheating. Was it as widespread as people often claimed? Were the results of that poll they took in class last month accurate? Back in high school, he'd cheated in one French class, he remembered. But he never made a habit of it. His fraternity in college had a file of old papers which some of the brothers re-typed and handed in as their own work, but as far as he could remember, that wasn't very common.

What about the kids nowadays? Were they any different? He decided to stop into the school's professional library during his free period that morning and see whether he could find out anything more specific on the subject.

"Good morning, Walter," said Mrs. Grable, the school librarian, who was always pleased whenever one of the teachers came into the library. "We haven't seen much of you lately."

"Yes, I know," Cannon said. "I've been so busy preparing lessons and grading papers that I don't get nearly as much time for reading as I'd like."

"Isn't it a shame? We have such a good collection of books and periodicals here, but the teachers never take advantage of them. Why, I often think that some of the teachers aren't even aware that we have a library here. I've been meaning to speak to Mr. Cunningham about it."

"You probably should, Mrs. Grable," Cannon said politely.

"But what is it that you came in for, Walter? May I be of any help?"

With Mrs. Grable's help, Cannon was able to find several articles which contained information on the frequency of cheating among students.

One study by Knowlton and Hamerlynck in the *Journal of Educational Psychology* reported the incidence of cheating in two colleges, one a small, rural, liberal arts college, the other a large, metropolitan university. At one school 81% of the sample admitted cheating in college, and 46% admitted cheating during that semester. At the other college, out of 533 students questioned, 252 admitted to being "active cheaters" (they profited from the cheating); 87, "passive cheaters" (others profited from the cheating); and 185 stated that they did not cheat.[4]

In another study, before an honor system was introduced at a large university, the studies indicated that 81% of the 299 students sampled had engaged in cheating. Once the honors system had been well-established, the degree of cheating dropped to "only" 30%.[5]

Cannon read two more studies which reported similar findings. Then Mrs. Grable came over to him with a magazine in her hand.

"I don't know if this will be of interest to you, Walter, but there's an article here which talks about some of the pressures which lead students to cheat or to work mainly for grades."

Mr. Cannon thanked her and took the article. The author began by quoting, at length, from a commercial publisher's advertisement for a study aid designed to help students get higher grades:

The old cliche says, "If you can't fight 'em, join 'em." Since there's no point in working at cross-purposes with your teacher, learn how to work with him.

Working with a teacher is not the same as apple-polishing. You have to work with people all your life, so start making a science of it.

Here are the major things to look for when studying a teacher:

What part of the course does he like best? What part does he like least? Watch out for small points that your teacher spends a lot of time on—he likes those points and they will probably be put on a test.

Does he like arguments in the classroom? Try yours out. Bring up a question that contradicts one of his own statements. If he likes it, do it again. If he doesn't, keep quiet when you disagree with him. There's no point irritating him.

What kind of tests does he give? Essay questions? True-false? Multiple choice? What kind of answers does he like? Good understanding of the main idea? Tiny details? You'll have to adjust your studying to his tests.

See if he has "good days" and "bad days." Don't

go out of your way to give your teacher a hard time
on his bad days.

Make a private appointment with your teacher. The
meeting can be helpful to both of you. He'll be glad
to see you, but be sure you have something specific
that you want to talk over since he may not have time
for just small talk.[6]

Cannon could hear MacIntyre's words coming back
to him: "If a teacher liked Toynbee, I gave him some
Toynbee on every exam." He read on.

At one university, 69% of the 185 students surveyed thought they sacrificed scholarship for grades.[7]

"I don't doubt it," thought Mr. Cannon.
Next, the author quoted a cartoon by Jules Feiffer:

"In the school I used to go to, I got *A*'s in all my
tests . . . And all the kids would ask me, 'How did
you do it, Joey?' . . . And I told them, 'I studied.' . . .
so they wouldn't play with me anymore. 'The Brain!'
they called me. 'The Professor!' . . . Even my father!
'I want you to be a normal American Boy!' he yelled
at me . . . So we moved away in disgrace.

Now in the new school I go to I still get *A*'s in all
my tests . . . And all the kids still ask me, 'How do
you do it, Joey?' But now I tell them, 'I cheated!'

It's great to be thought of as regular."[8]

Next, came a poem. Apparently the author of the
article had intended to create a collage—a collection of
material that illustrates pressures students are under to

pursue, relentlessly, high grades and even to cheat.

END OF A SEMESTER

This is the week of tests the season of fear
everywhere the running the typing the scritchscratch
shuffling of papers the door and the people
coming going looking for the symbols
looking for the little symbols written on the papers
stuck with tape to doors and walls
this is the week of the fearhope swallowed in
      the stomach
a time of livingdying a time of cominggoing
a time of inbetween the things one cannot grasp
too fast too fast we never sleep
we only keep ongoing

and somewhere someone in a great office
pushing buttons marking papers calling telephones
we think a devil who we cannot see is laughing.

and all the things we knew were true
will never do will never do
we all are weak we all are strong
the days are long the days are long

this is the week of tests the season of fear
somewhere we think a devil who we cannot see
      is laughing."

Then came an excerpt from a letter written "From the
Dean of Faculty" "To The Members Of The Faculty" of

a large, metropolitan university. The subject—CHEATING.

> . . . No single device or set of devices can elimi-
> nate cheating, but certain safeguards are available
> and essential. Whenever possible, students should be
> placed in alternate seats during tests, and all tests,
> including finals examinations, should be conscien-
> tiously proctored . . . The war against plagarism is
> never-ending, and every faculty member should bear
> in mind the possibility of plagarism when reading
> work prepared outside of class. Finally, examination
> questions should not be repeated on subsequent ex-
> aminations, for on every college campus various stu-
> dent groups keep back-files of old examinations. By
> the same token the same test should not be given
> to two or more sections of the same class, for students
> in the first section can always be relied on to tell the
> questions to some students in the other sections.
>
> I wish to apologize for sending this letter, for I am
> certain that almost all of you are aware of the
> problem and are handling it with both skill and suc-
> cess. On the other hand, I am convinced that if
> every faculty member assumes a firm stance against
> cheating, there will be a marked rise in student morale
> and a corresponding improvement in the educational
> enterprise to which we are all committed." [10]

"Educational enterprise, my eye," Cannon said to himself. "Those precautions sound more like they come out of a maximum security prison."

Shocked, dismayed and disgusted, Cannon gathered

together his papers and prepared to leave. Even if he had the strength to read on, he didn't have the time because the bell ending the third period was about to sound, and his forth period American history class was coming up.

"Come again, Walter," Mrs. Grable said, smiling as she took the magazines Cannon returned to her on the way out. "And weren't those two advertisements something—the ones at the end of that article?"

"I guess I didn't see them," Cannon said.

"Oh, you really *should*," Mrs. Grable said. "It'll just take a minute . . . Here they are."

> WANTED TO BUY top quality "A" graded term papers in all areas of the following disciplines: economics, political science, psychology, sociology, anthropology, philosophy, history, English, classics, geography. GR 6-4874, 9 a.m.-5 p.m.[11]

> $15 EACH—"A" Term Papers—1-any topic. Abnormal psych or 2-psych of Violence or 3-Juvenile Delinquency. With Biblio. Call 251-3733, Tues/Thurs. after 1 p.m.[12]

Cannon did not say good-bye to Mrs. Grable when he left the library, nor did he notice Miss Doyle's friendly wink as he passed her in the corridor. He walked pensively through the crowded, noisy hall to his classroom. He sat down in his chair, propped his feet up on the desk and mulled over all he had just read, awaiting the arrival of his students.

"You look like you're solving the problems of the world," Beth Sachs said, as she entered the classroom. Receiving no answer, she shrugged her shoulders and went over to talk to her friend Alice Mae Horton.

When the bell rang signaling the start of class, Barry Binson raised his hand and called out, "Mr. Cannon," as several of the boys around him made noises for people to be quiet.

"Yes, Barry."

"Well, Mr. Cannon, several of us were talking after yesterday's class, you know, when we decided to do something about the school's grading system . . ."

"Uh-huh," Cannon said, encouraging the boy to continue.

"Well, we began thinking how it might be a good idea to kind of, maybe, try something different in this class." (No one understood why Mr. Cannon smiled at this point.)"What I mean is, if we're going to get anywhere in this school, we've got to start someplace. And since most of us here are against grades, well, this would be a good place to start."

Barry fell silent and one of his buddies took over.

"In other words, Mr. Cannon, we're asking if you'd be willing to get away from the old grading system here in this class. We're all pretty interested in our work so I don't think anybody's gonna goof off or anything. I mean, if we can't do something here, we might as well forget about the rest of the school." Several students nodded their heads in agreement, while the rest of the class looked on with interest.

Finally, Terry Hansen said, "What do *you* think about grades, Mr. Cannon?" Every student waited for the teacher's reaction. He waited a long time before answering, and when he spoke, he spoke slowly.

"I was just looking up some research in the professional library downstairs. I wanted to see whether this talk about cheating and grade-grubbing was exaggerated, and I found out it isn't.

"I'm getting tired of running a classroom in which everything we do revolves around grades. I'm tired of being suspicious when students give me compliments, wondering whether or not they are just trying to raise their grade. I'm tired of spending so much time and energy grading your papers, when there are probably a dozen more productive and enjoyable ways for all of us to handle the evaluation of papers. I'm tired of hearing you ask me 'Does this count?' And, heaven knows, I'm certainly tired of all those little arguments and disagreements we get into concerning marks which take so much fun out of the teaching and the learning here at Mapleton High. To answer your question more directly, Terry, if we can come up with a better way than the present one for giving grades in this class, I'd not only be willing, I'd be downright happy to give it a try."

In any other setting, the class might have applauded, but this was a classroom, so they managed to contain themselves.

"I told you he'd go along with us," Barry Binson said

to Terry Hansen.

"It's *true* what he said," Maria Rivera said. "I *am* embarrassed to give him a compliment, because he might think I'm brown-nosing."

"Wowie, I can't wait to get started!"

"Boy, wait till the other classes hear about this."

"It'll never work."

"Who cares? It's worth a try."

"We're gonna turn this school upside down!"

But a few of the more thoughtful students brought the class back to reality.

"Hey, everybody, hold on. All Mr. Cannon just said was that he was willing to try something different in this class. He didn't say what, and we haven't come up with any specific ideas. So before we proclaim the Revolution, maybe we'd better think of what we're going to do in this class about grading."

"Why do we have to have grades at all?" asked one boy.

"Because the school says we have to," said another. "Isn't that right, Mr. Cannon?"

"That's true. I have to put something down on your IBM cards."

"What about putting down 'pass' or 'fail,' " suggested June Parelli. "My sister takes a couple of pass/fail courses in college, and she says they're really good. The teacher sets the minimum standards for passing and makes them very clear. Every student knows what she has to do to pass, and there's no anxiety about grades, except for the few, maybe, who are right on the border-line. There's much less cheating because, again, unless you need to cheat in order to pass, there's no reason for it."

June's suggestion captured the class' interest. Ideas flew back and forth, with students offering their personal reasons why they would like pass/fail grading.

"I'm sorry to throw a wet blanket on this," Cannon said. "There *is* a P on the IBM card, but we don't use it at present. You might want to suggest pass/fail grading when we talk about the school-wide changes you'd like to make, but for now, I'm afraid we have to stay within the limits of using the usual letters."

Accepting these boundaries, the class set to work deciding the grading system to be used in Cannon's class. Cannon was a skilled leader of the discussion. First he employed the brainstorming method in asking for all the possible ways of grading which they might use. No matter what plan each student suggested, even if it appeared foolish to him or the others, Cannon would list it on the board—the evaluation of each idea would come later. He said that criticizing after each suggestion would put a damper on people's imagination.

Those who had possible alternatives to suggest were heard from before the bell rang signaling the end of class, but no one made a move to leave. Everything was quiet, and the echo of the bell bounced from the back bulletin board up to the chalk board.

Ed Hecht said, "Wow, we really did a lot this period."

"But, man, we're still nowhere," Terry Hansen said.

"I'm satisfied we're on our way," Cannon said. "Let's pick up here tomorrow. Ed, will you get this stuff copied and put back on the board for us when you come in tomorrow?" Ed nodded.

The class filed out thoughtfully, without their usual chattering. Cannon erased the board. Students from his next class began wandering in, noisily unaware of what had happened.

The next morning, Ed was waiting at the door for the classes to change. When the bell rang, he slipped into the classroom before the first student to leave had even gotten to the door. He began copying their list of ideas on the chalkboard.

"Looks pretty good, huh, Mr. Cannon?" Ed asked.

"Well, we'll see, Ed. We'll see."

The students had obviously been thinking and talking about what had happened the day before. Cannon was full of anticipation. This was the kind of teaching he liked—so different from asking questions to which he already had one right answer in mind. The answer was out there in the future, and no teacher could know what it was—not like the four major causes of the Civil War. Cannon smiled and thought "Hell, I won't even be able to get a multiple-choice question out of today's class."

"Well, everybody, let's get at it. You've had the night to get your thoughts together, so let's hear them."

The class was full of animation and good spirits. The advocates of some form of self-grading started off. They felt that self-grading would take the friction out of the student-teacher relationship and would give each student the responsibility for setting his own standards and goals. Ned Fusari concisely justified this plan: "The responsibility for one's own learning is what life is all about anyhow."

"Will students be honest, though, Ned?" Jane Southern asked.

"It's no worse than what we've got now," Ned said.

Some students felt that the self-grade should be combined with a teacher grade and, maybe, a peer grade, averaged together. This would guard against a student's grading himself too high.

Terry Hansen was the spokesman for the "blanket grade" point of view.

"I feel that blanket grades would completely eliminate anxiety and competition within this class and would allow us to concentrate on *learning*. I, personally, think the blanket grade should be *C* but I know some other people in here want it to be a *B* and one nut told me 'why not all *A*'s as long as you're giving out Christmas presents in June?'" The class laughed.

Terry continued. "Another big advantage to the blanket grade of *C* would be to make a protest statement to the rest of the school as well. Our point that we don't agree with the present grading system would be made, and, by the same token, no one could accuse us of trying to get something for nothing."

"So why not a blanket *F*?" Joey Masters asked.

"I want to protest, not commit suicide!" Terry exclaimed, and Joey laughed.

Advocates of the contract system—grading according to differential work 'requirements set by the teacher—argued that their plan would eliminate anxiety from grading, too, but would give some meaning to the old system, and not just throw it out altogether.

They were in the middle of going back and forth on that plan when the bell caught them again. "O.K.," Cannon said, "we'll get back to this tomorrow. Don't lose faith. Decisions come hard when you're playing with real issues. See you tomorrow."

Well-thought-out ideas were rapidly offered the next day. Most students were against all of the plans put forth so far. Many students felt they would never grade themselves objectively, and they also did not trust their peers to grade them fairly either.

The blanket *A* was criticized as not being fair to other classes and it also allowed someone who might do no work to still get an *A*. The latter point, of course, was said of the blanket *B* and the "quilt *C*" (as Joey called it.).

Betty Stone said, "The blanket *B* or *C* would be unfair to those students who wanted or needed an *A* or a *B* to keep up their averages." Her comment made the class silent for a moment. Given the present system, this was an important consideration.

Art Fields was against the contract system and was quite eloquent in his arguments. "I don't see where the contracts do anything to eliminate competition. In fact, 'there will be *more* students at each other's throats, if you ask me. We'll have kids contracting and working for *A*'s even if they don't want them. That's the way it will turn out."

Finally, all the pros and cons had been aired. Cannon suggested that before they begin the most difficult part of their job—choosing the best alternative or finding a new one—they ought to list on the board the qualities they would like to see reflected by their final choice.

Our Grading System Should—

1. Eliminate the anxiety which usually goes with grading;
2. Create a relaxed learning atmosphere in the class;
3. Decrease competition for grades among students;
4. Be meaningful. That is, a student's grade should mean something to him, personally.
5. Respect quality of work, as well as quantity;
6. Allow those students who needed a high grade to get one.

The next day, surprisingly enough, the decision came quite quickly. Cannon believed that the process they had gone through during the first three days enabled each student to hear all sides of every suggestion, to present all his arguments to the class, to weigh the evidence and reach his own conclusion. The final choice was a variation of #11 from their brainstorming list of the first day: Everyone who does the work gets a *B;* teacher sets extra work requirement for an *A*.

"Well, fellow classmates," Terry said jokingly, "we might not have learned much history this week, but I'd like to feel that we just might have made a little."

According to their final choice, Cannon would set minimum standards for the quantity and quality of work that each student was expected to do. These would be spelled out very clearly, so every student would understand what was expected of him. The standards would be such that any student in the class, who applied himself, could meet them. All students who met the standards would receive a *B*. Any student who failed to meet these standards would receive an *F*. (In this sense, this could be called a *B* or fail system, very similar to pass/fail grading.) A student who handed in very poor work could redo the work as many times as he wanted to to bring it up to the established standards. For those students who felt they needed or wanted an *A*, the teacher would set an extra work requirement, and any student who completed this extra requirement, in addition to the basic requirements, would receive an *A*.

The whole process of brainstorming, evaluating and choosing a plan had taken four class periods. At times the students had felt excited during the discussion, and at times, frustrated and bored. But to see their faces when the decision was finally reached would be affirmation enough of how group decision-making affects the group's attitude toward the outcome.[13] Almost every member of the class felt he had played a part in the decision. Almost every member believed that, although the solution was by no means perfect nor sure to succeed, it was the best their collective wisdom could reach and, by golly, it was worth a try. As with all change, though, not everyone agreed.

"I still say I would rather have Mr. Cannon grade us as usual," Mary Ellen Wheeler and Jerry Szymanski said.

Art Fields said, like old Benjamin in *Animal Farm*, "I don't care what you do. Nothing will change. School will still be a waste of time."

But the plan had the enthusiastic support of the rest of the class, including Cannon. "Once we made that decision," he told Joyce later, "I felt I could breathe more freely than I have in eight years of teaching. The kids were excited and so was I. There was that feeling that something special was happening in the classroom. You know, where the kids for once realize that *they* have some control over their lives, over their education. That schools don't have to be factories. That they can work together, instead of cutting each other's throats. By making this decision today, we became a real group."

8 | To "B" or Not to "B"

DEPENDING ON the time of day, the <u>men's faculty room</u> could get quite crowded and noisy. First period, of course, was pretty tame; almost everyone had a class to teach. On the other hand, fourth period was often "standing room only."

In their faculty room, the men loosened their ties. Those who brought lunch with them had their feet up on the coffee tables, with the wax paper from their sandwiches spread out on their laps. The smokers tended to stick in one corner, but the whole room was gray and hazy when it got crowded. Once, a new student had pulled the fire alarm because he had seen all the smoke curling out from the crack in the bottom of the door of the men's faculty room.

There were always more copies of the *Daily News* scattered around than one might expect. Often the political talk was right out of its editorial pages. Sometimes the talk was about money or about sex, but sports predominated. Sometimes movies were discussed, complaints about students and administration were aired, and, occasionally, an idea about education came up Generally, shoptalk was frowned upon during these precious free periods.

This day, however, was an exception. The grading controversy had, for the most part, died down since MacIntyre's speech; but a new issue of the *Mapleton High Herald,* which had been distributed that morning, printed a full page of letters written in response to MacIntyre's speech. Charles Ingles, Henry Crewson, Biff Johnson, and Robert Jeffreys were hunched over a table reading some of the letters.

To the Editor:

I believe that Robert MacIntyre's speech was exaggerated, unfair, and uncalled-for. I am in school to get a good education. My teachers know a lot more than I do about what kinds of skills and knowledge are necessary for me to succeed later on in college. The existence of grades motivates me to do the work they feel will be helpful *to me,* so by working for a grade, I am really learning the things I need to know and, therefore, getting a good education.

I think we should be grateful for the opportunity to get a good education and to go to a school like Mapleton High School. There are a lot of places in this world where children do not have such an opportunity. All the teachers I know mark students fairly, and they get what they deserve.

Jeffrey Stevenson

"I'd almost be willing to take a salary cut," Charles Ingles said, "if I could have more students like that boy. He did a great job in my chemistry class last year. I wrote a good recommendation to Dartmouth for him a few weeks ago. He'll probably get in too."

"He probably will," said Biff Johnson from Physical Education. "I bet it won't hurt his average any when his teachers read this letter of his."

Henry Crewson, a social studies teacher, frowned at Biff Johnson, and the teachers continued reading the letters.

> Dear Editor,
>   Grades aren't fair. I have a teacher who doesn't like me, and I know she takes extra points off on my tests because of it. On our last test, I had almost the exact same answer on a 20-point essay question as another student in my class. But I got 3 points less. When I told the teacher, she said I shouldn't worry about what anyone else got, but I should be concerned about improving my own work. But if I try to improve, she'll just take off extra points anyway.
>
>   (name withheld upon request)

"Bah, I'm tired of hearing these kids' sob stories," Henry Crewson said. "I wish they'd stop making excuses for their own failures and face up to the facts like that Stevenson boy does."

"Well, I don't know about that, Henry," Charles Ingles said. "My daughter had a similar experience in *her* high school.[1] Her English teacher gave the class an interpretive essay for the mid-term and gave my daughter a 69.5. I looked it over myself, and it wasn't badly written. But the teacher said her 'development' was poor. Well, it seems a lot of the other kids had the same complaint, so the next day some of them went down to their guidance officer to complain. Naturally, he couldn't do anything and suggested that the kids talk it over with their teacher.

"My daughter talked to the teacher, but she wouldn't change her mind. So she went to the head of the English department who said he'd talk to the teacher. Of course, nothing was done. In fact, when the teacher heard that some of the kids complained, she refused to discuss the marks anymore with anyone. My kid had two *A*'s and now this *D* on the mid-term, so she'll get a *B*. She was furious, poor kid, and I don't blame her one bit."

"Students and teachers sure do get into a lot of needless conflict over grading," said Robert Jeffreys, the first-year English teacher who had had trouble with his class over the grading of poetry. "It's enough to make you anti-grades."

Crewson withered him with a glance. "No it isn't," he said. "It's enough to make you opposed to those teachers who don't know how to use grades properly. More objectivity is what is needed, if you ask me."

Jeffreys looked down at the school paper. The four of them began reading again.

Dear Editor:
To start off with, I never did like the idea of grades. I first went to a private school where we didn't receive formal grades. I first got grades when I came here in the seventh grade.
I never thought in terms of grades even then, but

as the years passed, grades began to be important. Teachers talked about them, classmates and people out of school talked about them, and so did I, in time. I am now accustomed to grades and I believe they serve a purpose which a pass-fail system would not. When I get my evaluation and see a *C* rather than an *A*, I know I will have to work harder and, in turn, will learn more. But not if I was to see just a "pass." If, however, one was to only be graded by comments, that would be good. But, then again, if a teacher's comments were too concise, they would be as confining as a grade.

In time I feel it would be a good idea to abolish the grading system. But for now, I would like to have it the way it is. I know that if you want to change something, you have to begin somewhere; but I personally and maybe selfishly, don't want it to start while I'm in the middle.

Joanne Mallas[2]

"What's she saying?" asked Jeffreys. "Is she for or against grades? I can't tell."

"Looks to me like she has mixed feelings," said Biff Johnson. "I know I did when I was a kid. I hated grades. But I was scared to hell that if I didn't have any grades, I wouldn't do any work."

"It's not difficult to tell where these next two guys stand," Charles Ingles said.

Sir:

Grading is symptomatic of something deeply wrong with our educational values. Our schools should provide an atmosphere where students are free to explore and expand upon the urgings of their curiosity. Gaining an education should be a joy, characterized by the excitement of discovery. Instead, our schools have become a kind of proving ground, whose most pervasive feature is competition.

Grades have turned students away from a striving for knowledge to a striving for success. Creativity has been replaced by conformity as students seek desperately for the attitudes that will earn them the highest grades, for the answers that will please the teacher the most. In the struggle, integrity has been lost. Students are at war with each other, and any maneuver is valid if it will earn a higher grade. Grades must go.

Michael Bogin and Robert Madden[3]

As the men were finishing the last letter, Russ Collins came in, followed by Cliff Harper. Harper yanked the door open and used it like a fan. He mimed being choked and gassed by all the cigarette smoke.

"Ah, if only you guys had learned your science, you might be more concerned about polluting the air around here," he said.

"All right, Harper. Save the lecturing for your students."

"What, me lecture? You must be kidding. I'm very modern. I use the discovery method." Harper found a seat near the window which he opened wider.

"Well, Mr. Biology," Russ Collins said. "You may be the hot-shot about modern methods around here, but

Walt Cannon is really taking the lead in evaluting. Did the rest of you hear that he's going to give everybody in his history class a blanket *B?* I just heard it today from one of his students."

The other conversations that had started up in the room broke off. Crewson, the most conservative member of Cannon's department, said, "What? A blanket *B?*"

"Yeah, the same grade for every kid in the class, and the grade is a *B.*"

"No matter how much work they do?"

"You got it, or at least that's what I heard he was going to do."

Crewson's interest swelled. "Let me get this straight. No matter how well they do on quizzes, or reports, or papers or examinations?" His pitch rose with incredulity as he mentioned each item.

Biff Johnson was about to bait Crewson with, "And why not?" but Lawrence Kelly, who had come in during the course of the conversation, said it for him.

"And why not? I'm getting a little weary myself spending half of my teaching life making up little true and false questions, running off the dittoed exams and burning all that midnight oil with a red pencil in my hand. I think maybe Cannon has something there."

"Wait a minute, Larry. Just wait a minute," said Russ Collins, who was known to be the hardest marker in Mapleton High. "You can't go around giving out grades like they were relief checks. Not everyone is equal. No everyone has the same worth. I wouldn't be doing my duty, nor deserve the right to be called a teacher, if I ignored my responsibilities about marks. Oh, sure, they're abused sometimes, but a real teacher will learn how to use them; and he must evaluate his students and grade them on what they have produced, what they . . ."

"Can vomit back to you when you demand that they puke it up?" Harper cut in.

"Look, Harper," Crewson said, "You don't have to be vulgar to maintain your popularity with students; and you're not going to make me defensive about the high standards I have and always will have. Nobody, by God, will ever get a *B* from me who hasn't earned it!"

"I'm in full agreement with you, Henry," Ingles said. "I figure I've recorded probably 12,000 grades during my teaching career, and I'm really proud about the objectivity of my grading. Numbers don't lie; and when I tote them up in that rollbook, any student can check my math and see that he's gotten just what he worked for."

Biff Johnson looked up from his *Daily News.* "Only whores get just what they work for, Charlie."

Crewson, trying to ignore Johnson's flip comment, added, "One thing you'll learn when you've taught as long as I have: Kids will work for grades, and they won't work without them. It's as simple as that."

"It's true," Charles Ingles said, "Without a little threatening, they won't do the unpleasant work that has to be done."

Johnson put his paper down again and spoke over it.

"But what makes *you* do the unpleasant work *you* have to do, Charlie?" he asked.

"I do it because I have a deep sense of responsibility, Biff. I wish every teacher realized that there is nothing inherently wrong with grades. The problems we have sometimes arise because some irresponsible teacher doesn't know how to grade properly. With a little effort, grading can be objective, fair and accurate. Now I admit, Jeffreys, grading *is* easier in Chem than it would be in English. And I do agree with your students that poetry is too subjective and should not be graded; but science and math, yes even history, can be measured, and a curve drawn. We can make the grading very accurate."

"I'm intrigued by your use of the word 'responsible,' Henry," Harper said. "If you were convinced that the giving of grades, no matter how carefully they were figured out, was basically an irresponsible thing to do to young people, would you quit giving grades?"

"Of course I would, and I would be sorely troubled by the 20 years of accurate grades I have given in the past. But frankly, Cliff, I don't have much worry about the guilt I'll have to live with. I can't conceive of anyone's convincing me that grading is, indeed, irresponsible. This is a competitive society, I would remind you, and all through their lives, our students are going to be graded. They are going to be graded to get into college, and all through college, and graduate school, and by their superiors on their first job and every job they'll ever get

Grades are a part of life, and to remove them would be to make the school even less relevant than the militants claim it is already.

"I'm not at all moved by that 'Life is hard' stuff," Harper responded. "Yes, grades are a part of life, as are heroin and graft and illegitimate babies, but I feel that some parts of life can be changed with my help, so I want to at least try."

"Harper has a point there," Jeffreys said. "One of my professors last year used to say that this is also a cooperative world we live in, and if we don't start teaching our students how to cooperate, we just may annihilate each other right off this earth."

"You and Harper are a bit melodramatic," Crewson said. "The big point is that we must teach responsibility. In fact, this may be the most important thing we can teach anyone. I simply believe that grades contribute to developing that sense of responsibility."

Biff Johnson flipped his *Daily News* over his shoulder and right into a wastebasket. He stood up to go. "That's a bunch of crap, Henry. I quit coaching because of nonsense like that. In the old days I was really sold on the idea that sports develop responsibility. Oh, how we hustled that good sportsmanship, building character, 'making men out of boys' junk.

"Don't you see? It's like that kid the other day said. Grades are just like sports. If you don't win, they don't let you play. But if you're going to win, you've got to learn how to hold the other team's jerseys so the ref won't see what you're doing. You've got to learn to use your elbows and knees, dirty-like, and how to rough up their quarterback badly enough so maybe he won't be able to finish the game! Responsibility my eye! Crewson, let me tell you something. You like grades because they give you *power* over trembling kids; and the more they tremble, the more power you feel. Responsibility? No. Power!" With that word, he walked out.

Crewson sighed. "Boy, he ought to do some more push-ups. He's getting a little soft."

"I'm not so sure," Harper said. "I think he really said something to all of us when he brought up that power issue. Well, I'm off to my fifth period class to ask them whether they want to consider the blanket *B* idea. A little blanket might warm us all up on these cold December days."

The bell rang raucously. Cigarettes were snuffed out and the men gathered up their papers and got ready to enter the flow of bodies moving towards fifth period classes.

9 | *The Principal and the Position Paper*

For Joseph Cunningham, principal of Mapleton High School, the New Year turned out to be one big headache, beginning the second week after the students were back.

Henry Crewson poked his head in Cunningham's office door and said, "Joe, I might as well tell you, Cannon's kids are not setting one foot in my classroom if they intend to stir up trouble. If I were you, I'd put a stop to this whole thing *right now.*" He produced a sheaf of papers from his coat pocket and threw them on the principal's desk. Then he said, "I'll talk to you later. I've got to get to class."

He left before Cunningham could open his mouth. Cunningham reached for the papers Crewson had given him and inwardly groaned as he read the words *Position Paper* on the first page. The Grading Committee of Mr. Cannon's fourth period class hadn't wasted any time.

Before leaving for Christmas vacation, Terry Hansen had suggested that the committee meet sometime during the vacation for a combined strategy planning meeting and party. The Committee liked the idea. Although some of them had to be away visiting grandparents or on ski trips and out-of-town vacations, ten people showed up for the planning party.

As it turned out, they never got to the party. They spent an hour discussing possible strategies. Everything from burning the grade records in the guidance office to writing a letter-to-the-editor of the *Herald* was suggested. In the end, they decided to write a clear and forceful position paper and circulate this paper through the entire school. Once they had built a substantial support base for their cause, they would decide what strategy would be best to get their recommendations implemented.

Once the position paper idea had been agreed upon, they split up into smaller groups to do the writing. Then they read their sections aloud, made changes, combined the various portions, arranged and re-arranged the sections and came up with a tentative draft of the paper. During the first week back in school, they showed the rest of the Committee their first draft, made additional changes and, feeling very proud of themselves, arrived at their final version.

It was one of a thousand copies the Committee had mimeographed that Mr. Cunningham sat at his desk reading.

POSITION PAPER

Before Robert MacIntyre's speech in the assembly last December, our fourth period history class had spent a considerable amount of time studying the history of grades and discussing grading and education at Mapleton High School. Our study of grading showed us that grading did not always exist and that its existence was never justified by sound educational reasons—only by historical convenience. After hearing Mr. MacIntyre's speech and discussing this important issue further, many of us became convinced that traditional grading was outdated and harmful to today's education.

What follows is our Position Paper on Grading at Mapleton High School:

1. WE BELIEVE GRADES HAVE BECOME MORE IMPORTANT TO STUDENTS THAN LEARNING.

This was the main point of Mr. MacIntyre's speech, and we agree with him. We care more about our grades than our education. Except in unusual circumstances, we don't study because we are interested in learning about something but because we want to get good grades on our tests. As long as grading exists and is so important in determining our futures, this situation will continue.

2. GRADES ENCOURAGE CHEATING.

Because grades have become so important, we feel pressured to get as good a grade as possible, whatever the method. There is a great deal of cheating at Mapleton High, as is true everywhere. Cheating takes many forms, but most students do cheat, and some of them, frequently. Cheating would be less prevalent, or perhaps non-existent, in a better educational system.

3. GRADES DIVIDE TEACHERS AND STUDENTS INTO WAR-
RING CAMPS.

We think teachers and students should work together in
school, but so often they are fighting each other. We are
all witnesses to, and sometimes participants in, apple-
polishing (brown-nosing) and trying to impress teachers
by talking a lot in class. Students feel uncomfortable
about giving a teacher a compliment, because the
teacher might be suspicious that the student is just trying
to improve his grade, or because other students will think
so. Too often, teachers and students spend valuable time
arguing about grades rather than about ideas. Instead of
learning together, teachers and students are fighting one
another every step of the way.

4. GRADES DISCOURAGE STUDENTS FROM DEVELOPING
THEIR OWN GOALS.

We find that we learn best when we are interested in
something, when we can pursue our own goals. But
grades are so important that we have to spend all our
time doing what the teachers want us to. So we learn
to adopt other people's goals and do what they want us
to do, but we don't get a real chance to find out what *we*
want and what interests *us*. When we can choose between
courses, some of us take those which will be easier or
which have a teacher who is an easy marker. This decision is made even though there may be other courses
that we think we would get more out of. It's not the

students' fault; it's the fault of grading.

5. GRADING STIFLES CREATIVITY.

Once you figure out (it's usually pretty easy) what a teacher wants, you stand a better chance of getting a good grade. But to be creative you have to do something in an original way. Sometimes the teacher might not understand what you're trying to do, or he might not like it, and then your grade suffers. So most students play it safe and don't run the risk of getting a low grade by trying something creative.

6. GRADES ARE NOT APPLIED FAIRLY.

Some teachers are hard markers and some are easy. This doesn't seem fair. An *A* or a *B* or a *C* should mean the same thing no matter which teacher uses it.

Also, some teachers, not *all,* are not objective about their students. They play favorites. Some teachers are prejudiced against students who disagree with them, others against students who have bad reputations or wear their hair long or all sorts of other ridiculous reasons.

7. GRADES CREATE AN UNHEALTHY ATMOSPHERE IN THE SCHOOL.

We are forced to compete with one another for grades, creating jealousy, and making us unwilling to help another classmate with his work. Too much tension and anxiety exists among students because we are so worried about passing, about getting good grades, about getting into college. School isn't an enjoyable place; it's like a rat race and we're the rats.

8. GRADES SUPPORT THE OTHER PROBLEMS IN SCHOOL.

Grading isn't the only problem in school. The homework assignments and the classroom discussions are often dull and meaningless. Free expression is often frowned upon; the teaching usually needs to be improved; and some of the courses seem out-dated. But poor teaching is often covered up by giving students low grades and making them think their lack of knowledge is their own fault. Without the threatening aspects of being graded, students would have more freedom to try to change some of the other problems in the school. For example, they could examine with a teacher the possibility that a particular assignment might be a waste of time. They would not have to fear that by saying what they believe and standing up for their rights, they would be jeopardizing their grade average.

Recommendation

The members of our class committee would like to recommend that our school change the traditional grading process to a pass/fail system of grading, as mentioned by Mr. Robert MacIntyre in his speech. Under this new system, the teacher would set up at the beginning of the semester his requirements for passing, and then anyone who fulfilled these would pass. The requirements should be set up so that any student who works hard at a subject would pass. Two of the members of our class have a brother and a sister in college and they each have pass/fail courses. Both said that almost everybody still works, and what is as important, if not more so, the students are more relaxed, and seem to learn more, and the classes are much more interesting.

We hope this recommendation can be acted upon as soon as possible.

Mr. Cunningham was beginning to understand what Crewson was complaining about. But he still didn't know how the *Position Paper* was being circulated.

Upon returning from vacation, each student on the grading committee selected and approached one history teacher who knew him well and who trusted him. After briefly explaining the class' project to the teacher, the student asked for permission to have a few members of the committee visit the classes of that teacher to present and discuss the *Position Paper* with the students. It was a clever and workable plan. Since they had approached only history teachers, they avoided the problem of visiting classes where they would keep running into the same students. And since the committee members had asked only teachers who knew and trusted them, a majority of the teachers had agreed to give up class time for the committee to speak. The main problem was finding those times when the members of the grading committee had free time themselves to visit the other classes. By using their regularly scheduled history class time, study and also lunch periods, and the class time that other sympathetic teachers allowed them to miss and make up, "Cannon's 17" was able to contact directly about three-quarters of the student body.

Generally, three members of the committee would try to attend each visit to another class. The spokesman for the group on that occasion would explain how their history class had become interested in the subject of grading, how they had done a unit on the history of grading and education, how they had been moved by Mr. MacIntyre's speech, and how they had decided to undertake a project to *do something* about the school's grading system. Then they handed out copies of their *Position Paper* to the class, gave them time to read it through, and proceeded to lead a discussion.

The discussions were always lively. Very few students in the school did not care passionately—one way or another—about the subject of grading. Grades seemed to have relevance to everyone, including the history teachers who were sometimes the most vocal discussants of all. Teachers and students alike were divided on the issues. Arguments flared up in the classrooms and spilled over into the halls, the cafeteria and even to other classrooms. Within two weeks, just about every student and teacher in the school had seen and read a copy of the *Position Paper*. Even if they had not participated in a discussion led by some of Cannon's students, they had undoubtedly argued about the grading issue with other students, other teachers and their parents.

Naturally, the *Position Paper* found its way into the hands of parents and citizens within the community of Mapleton. Almost instantly, parents were calling Cunningham, or the Superintendent or members of the school board to express their protest or support.

To top it off, the whole issue came right in the midst of studying for midterms. The class committee had taken into consideration whether this would be the most opportune time to make their move, and had debated both sides of the question. One argument was that, since the students' thoughts and energies were so involved in studying for their exams, they would not be able to get interested or involved in the grading question. The other argument was that since the students would be, *at that very time,* sweating under the pressures of the grading system, the weeks just prior to midterms would be the perfect time to raise the issue. They decided to act immediately.

"Join us, Mr. Cunningham," Doris Doyle said. "The natives are restless today, and we need a little comfort from our leader." Cunningham put down his aluminum tray and carefully removed the weight-watcher's salad.

"This grading business is making everyone high as a kite," Mrs. Wagner said. "It took me twenty minutes to get my girls down to business and to start working. We were making carrot and raisin salad. You know how you have to grate the carrots? Well, somehow they all thought it was very funny to keep asking each other what "grate" they were going to give their carrots when they evaluated them."

"Actually, I think that's kind of cute," Miss Doyle said.

"Oh, it was cute enough, but not for 20 minutes," Mrs. Wagner said.

"Grades seem to be the topic of discussion everywhere this morning," Miss Heath said. "A couple of those intellectual girls from one of Harper's classes wanted to know if they would get extra credit for taking two showers after gym. I think they were baiting me. Another one wanted to know if she would lose points for having her period in the middle of the parallel bars exercise."

"These are creative kids," Miss Doyle said. "A lot more lively than we used to be."

"Well, I just wish they were a little less lively," Mrs. Wagner said. "Instead of all this talk of doing *away* with grades, I think we could control students better if we moved towards a number system, 0-100, the way *we* had it in school. Then perhaps there would be more discipline around this place."

Cunningham looked at her. "Mrs. Wagner, you're not saying that the office doesn't back you up when you have a discipline problem are you?"

"Oh, not *that*, Mr. Cunningham. Don't get me wrong.

I guess the students, especially the girls, are just harder
to teach today than they used to be. They're, well, they're
so unafraid."

"Life is so ludicrous," Miss Doyle added. "We used to
gripe about how apathetic the kids were, and now that
they're showing a little spirit, we don't like that either.
As for me, I'm very excited about this grading controversy at Mapleton High. It's the best thing that has
happened since we won the sectional championship in
basketball. I'm really glad to see the kids unapathetic for
a change."

"I agree with you, Doris," Miss Heath said, "but Rose
has a point, too. I like to see them unapathetic, as you
call it, too, but just not quite so much so." She looked
to Cunningham. He was nodding his approval.

The door swung open. Cliff Harper stood there holding it with his back so that Walter Cannon, Robert
Jeffreys and Biff Johnson could come in also.

"Ah, Mr. Cunningham. Just the man we've been looking for," Biff said. "Good morning to you, ladies. Do you
have room for the four of us?"

"With the food you have piled on that tray, Biff, you
may need a table just for yourself," Miss Doyle teased.

"Training table regulations, my dear. A sound mind
in a sound body."

"What's on you minds, men?" Cunningham asked.
"You look like you've been having a little caucus."

"You're right, boss," Harper answered. "It's grades.
They are on everyone's mind. It's really becoming a big

issue with the kids, as I'm sure you've picked up, and I'm getting a little embarrassed about their carrying the ball while we seem to sit idly by."

Biff Johnson joined in. "Shouldn't we have a faculty meeting so we could formally discuss this grading matter to see how we all feel about it? I've just been getting pieces here and there and a hell of a lot of rumors everywhere."

"I see your point, Biff," Cunningham said, "but you know that the next two faculty meetings are scheduled and the agendas are already overloaded. Remember, the accrediting business starts next year and we've just got to get that thing organized."

Jeffreys started to raise his hand as if he expected to be called on in class, then he asked, "Sir, do they ever call special faculty meetings here at Mapleton? You know, a meeting to deal just with one important issue which comes up."

"Yes, well, we've done that in the past, but only when some emergency arose. The faculty doesn't like to meet for more than the scheduled meetings."

"Look, Joe," Harper said to the principal, "I think you're going to have to call a lot more special meetings regarding this grading issue if we don't face it soon. Besides, I'd hate to see the SDS kids tie you up in your swivel chair and set fire to your file cabinets!" There was a tender twinkle in Harper's eyes as he said this.

Cunningham scraped the bottom of his yogurt cup.

"We'll see about *that*. I certainly don't want a civil war breaking out around here." He thought to himself a moment, then said. "All right. Maybe you're right. Why don't I call a professor I know who has done a lot of work on evaluation? I'll ask him to come to a special meeting. We'll give the topic of grading the priority. This professor will air the research, tell us what the literature says, and so forth. Having him give us some of the facts will lend some dignity to our own deliberations. Then after his presentation, we can set up some buzz groups, combining those who are either pro or con. Then we'll wind up the meeting with some reports from each group so we all know where we stand. How does that sound?"

"Sounds like an interesting afternoon," Biff said. "When will it be?"

"Oh, I don't think there's any great rush. How about next month sometime? That will give me time to contact the consultant and will enable us to organize the meeting properly."

"I wouldn't wait that long, Joe," Harper gently warned him.

Back in his office, Joe Cunningham saw message slips for five phone calls he was supposed to return. His secretary, Mrs. Reynolds, said, "They were all hot-under-the-collar about this grading business. As far as I could gather, five out of five were strongly opposed to any changes being made in the present grading system."

"What a lovely way to begin an afternoon. Let's see

them, Claire. Hmm. Harry Hotchkiss. I think I'll face him last. Who's this one? Mrs. Fingert? I don't think I know her, do I? Oh, brother, Mrs. Sloane. I should have known that *that* crank would get in on this. O.K., I'll talk to these two first. Will you dial them for me, Claire? Thanks."

He went to his desk and dropped into the swivel chair, thinking what it would be like to be tied up in it. The light went on at the base of his phone. He hoped Claire was dialing Mrs. Herbert Hodges because she was an intelligent, reasonable woman. At least she had been in the past. She would be a good weather vane for what the community's thinking was about this grading issue.

The intercom buzzer rang. "Mrs. Hodges on 35, Mr. Cunningham," Claire reported.

"Thank you." Then with deliberation he pushed down the button marked 35. "Good afternoon, Mrs. Hodges. This is Joseph Cunningham. What can I do for you?"

"Well, I'm glad you called me back, Mr. Cunningham. I'm also glad I didn't get you the first time, since I'm a bit calmer now. I called because I heard the news that Mapleton High was slowly going to do away with grading and I want to know if that's so."

Cunningham sighed right into the phone. "That is a rumor you heard, Mrs. Hodges, and at present, a false one. We *are* spending some time talking about grading since, and I hope you'll agree, we feel the matter is worth investigation."

"Of course. But we didn't move out to Mapleton from the city just to discover that our son won't get into a first-rate college because Mapleton High might decide to experiment with some new grading system which may endanger his future academic career. Buying a home out here was a tremendous sacrifice, Mr. Cunningham, and we're not going to let changes which hurt our children go unnoticed."

"Now, now, Mrs. Hodges, you know me better than that. Some students and some faculty members have been *talking* about the advantages and disadvantages of grades, but that's as far as it has gone. You can rest assured that your Gerald will certainly complete his high school education at Mapleton High without any disadvantages to him. We all respect Gerald, Mrs. Hodges, and we know he will get into the college of his choice. We also know he has a bright future ahead of him."

"Well, Mr. Cunningham, I thank you for those nice words about Gerald, but I'm not talking about a *rumor*. The information which has caused Mr. Hodges and me such concern is, I'm afraid, much more than a rumor. Gerald told us he has two teachers who are giving every student a *B*, no matter how much studying each one does. I hope you are aware of this."

"Why, yes, Mrs. Hodges," Mr. Cunningham hedged, "but that doesn't mean the whole school is moving in that direction. In fact, we have a faculty meeting in two weeks to investigate the matter of grading. As a faculty, we make decisions which affect us all. No faculty member will be able to make unilateral decisions on important policy. Please call me back, say about the middle of the month, and please don't worry about Gerald. He's a fine boy and he'll do very well with his Mapleton High School preparation."

"Thank you, Mr. Cunningham. I certainly *will* call back. I appreciate your time and concern."

"Thank you, Mrs. Hodges. I enjoyed talking with you." Mr. Cunningham fingered the marble base to his pen set, then he rang for his secretary. "Claire, please get me Harry Hotchkiss now, instead of that other call. I better face him now."

Harry Hotchkiss was an old classmate of Cunningham's. They had trained together to become teachers, but Hotchkiss had never taught. Instead, he went into selling toys and then had started his own wholesale toy company and had done very well, financially. The principal and his old classmate were surfacy friends. There was an unspoken competitiveness between them. Joe Cunningham preferred to see Harry Hotchkiss as rarely as possible.

The phone rang, Cunningham picked it up.

"Joe, is that you? Listen, you old renegade, the whole town is buzzing about your encouraging the student militants, being soft on the faculty radicals and letting them run your school for you."

"Come on, Harry, tell me what they're really saying," Cunningham said, a note of impatience evident in his voice.

"Well, Joe, a bunch of the taxpayers are saying that you're giving some of their money to the far-out students for an underground newspaper, and for ditto paper to put out position papers designed to undermine Mapleton High. That's what they're saying, and after having seen one of those position papers, I'd say we have something more than rumor here, Joe. What's your side of it?"

"Harry, you could do me a big favor: read that *Position Paper*. Then do me another favor: tell everyone you meet that I'm not only *not* giving any money for an underground newspaper, we don't even *have* an underground newspaper and probably never will. Tell them that the good old *Mapleton High Herald* prints all the news that's fit to print. How's that?"

"Sure, Joe, sure. But I thought I'd better warn you that people are talking. Where there's smoke, there's fire. You better get your fire hoses ready, Joe. I'd hate to see you tied up in your swivel chair by those long-haired creeps while they ransack your office."

"You know what, Harry? You're the second guy who has tied me up in my swivel chair today. I don't know what's happening around here."

"I told you that you should have joined me in the toy racket, Joe, instead of wasting your talents running that baby-sitting shop. Well, give my regards to the wife. See you soon. Drop around for a drink."

"Sure, Harry, and thanks for calling. I appreciate your help." Cunningham hung up, thought for a minute, and then he rang for his secretary.

"Claire, give Harper a buzz and tell him I'm going to call the special faculty meeting for Friday of this week. Ask him to drop in on his way home tonight. Thanks, Claire. Oh, then get me a long distance line."

Cunningham was able to reach the professor. Yes, he would enjoy coming as a consultant to talk about evaluation, but this Friday was out of the question. Yes, he had a colleague he could recommend, even though it was on such short notice. No, he was a younger man and hadn't done much of this consulting business yet. Yes, he was a good man, and would do an excellent and scholarly job. In fact, the other professor just passed the office. He'd ask him. He'd save you a call. If you *don't* hear from him, the other professor will be there at 3:00 on Friday. Thanks for calling. Yes, he'll come another time if you invite him. Maybe in the spring, but this Friday is just impossible. Wish you had called earlier.

10 | *The Day the Consultant Came*

THE AFTERNOON SUN that Friday splashed through the big windows and painted the library with pale yellow streaks. Some of the teachers were already seated, and others were standing around the coffee table. Cunningham and Crewson entered the room with the speaker for the afternoon.

Trailing behind them were two boys from the audio-visual department, one carrying an overhead projector and the other wheeling in a cart on which sat a small, strange-looking gadget that resembled a miniature version of a computer, somewhat similar to those one might see on television during election night coverage.

Several teachers interrupted their conversations to question each other about what the equipment was for, but few of them moved to sit down.

Cunningham encouraged the last of the teachers to get their coffee and bring it to their seats. Then he called the meeting to order. After a few routine announcements, he explained why the special meeting had been called and then introduced the speaker for the afternoon.

Dr. Miller walked casually up to the lectern and began immediately in a very matter-of-fact, almost conversational tone.

"I'm very pleased to be here today," he began. "I haven't been fortunate enough to speak at many faculty meetings, and this is also the first opportunity I've had to try out this little portable computer with such a large group. I hope you're feeling experimental today and don't mind being guinea pigs for the next hour or so."

A few groans came from the audience, and several teachers, whispering, began to share their displeasure or curiosity with their neighbors. Dr. Miller turned his eyes to the lectern and studied the rather lively four-letter words carved into its surface. He smiled at the idea of reading aloud a few of them in order to grab the teachers' attention but, instead, he waited a few seconds, marveling at how some teachers could, without embarrassment, act just as they had told their own students not to act.

"I understand you've been looking into the issue of grades and marks at Mapleton High," he continued. "I'm going to give each of you one of these computer cards. Please don't mutilate, spindle, or, heaven forbid, fold them! I'm going to ask you some questions concerning your attitudes toward grading; then we'll run the cards through the computer and find out fairly quickly where the faculty stands on the issue."

Dr. Miller flashed on a transparency of the IBM card. "You'll notice that there is no place for your name. So, please be as honest as possible. I'm going to ask ten questions. When we're done, I'll run the cards through the computer. While they're being tabulated, I have another experiment which I think you'll find just as interesting. For that one, I'll need all of you to sit with your own department. So after everyone is finished with his card, please shift accordingly."

Dr. Miller turned back to the screen and explained that each of the questions required the teachers to consider a factor which they believed should or should not influence grading. "For example," he said, replacing the first transparency with the second one, "I might ask whether you think a student's race should affect his grade. You answer by coloring in one of the five possible responses printed on the card." His finger projected large and black on the screen and touched the scale to which he was referring:

TRANSPARENCY NO. 2—SCALE TO BE USED.

A. It would be very important to consider this item when grading.
B. Somewhat important.
C. I have no strong feeling either way.
D. Should not be considered very heavily when grading.
E. Definitely should not be considered at all when grading.

"Should we answer that question about race?"

"No. That was just an example," Dr. Miller said. Then he continued, in a much louder and more impersonal manner. "Number one: Do you think a student's IQ should be taken into consideration in his grade?" He had written each question on a separate transparency, and he placed each of them on the projector in the order he asked them.

"Number two," he said, ignoring a teacher's raised hand. "Should final exams be taken into consideration when grading at the end of the semester?

"Number three: Should effort play a part in a student's grade?

Many teachers still eyed him quizzically, but he continued.

"Four: Where do you stand on a monthly test—or at least one large test for each marking period?

"Five: Do you think a student's popularity with other students should affect his grade?"

The young professor paused and waited for all the teachers to catch up. Periodically, one or two of them glanced up at the screen or chewed nervously on the end of his pencil before marking the card in front of him. Dr. Miller couldn't be sure what the teachers were feeling, but they seemed involved.

"Number six: Should class participation be considered in the grade?

"Seven: Is the student's social class a factor?

"Eight: Should the student's ability to give you back exactly the same answers you want be considered?"

A few ironic chuckles rippled across the room, but Dr. Miller kept going.

"Nine: Should the student's courage to take issue with what you say, to argue and sometimes prove you wrong, be considered?

"And the last one: Where do you stand on the idea of a grading curve—an equal number of people receiving low grades and high grades?"

When he had finished, his ten questions, as well as the rating scale, were shown on the screen. Dr. Miller gave the teachers another minute or two to check their answers and then asked that all the cards be passed forward. The room was quietly buzzing as teachers discussed the various questions the professor had posed. When the teachers were grouped together by departments and had settled themselves in their chairs, Dr. Miller tapped for attention.

"Through the light-fingered efforts of some of my student-teachers, I have obtained and have mimeographed various test papers, actually written by students from other schools in this city. I'm going to give all the members of each department the same paper to grade. Thus, history teachers will grade a history paper; science teachers, a science exam; and so on. You grade the paper as though it had been written especially for you. The idea, of course, is to see just how close your marks will be to those of your colleagues. Does anyone care to make a prediction?"

Ingles seemed to come to life for the first time that afternoon. "I bet the English teachers will have a spread of about 30 points but those of us in math and science will be within 5 points of each other, right down the line."

The English teachers stirred uncomfortably in their seats, and the math and science teachers sat up a little straighter and grinned at one another.

"Well, that should be interesting to find out, sir," Dr. Miller said, smiling. "Is everyone ready? Remember, consider this test paper a real one and grade it as you would any one of your students'."

The large room grew silent; only the sounds of turning pages and the efficient clicking of the little computer could be heard.

"Finish up now." Dr. Miller's sharp voice sliced through the silence. "Actually, I've given you about twice as long as you would have taken had you had a whole stack of papers in front of you.

"Now, put a grade at the top of the paper," Dr. Miller told them, "but not your name, and hand them in, face down. One person from each table please collect them and trade them for a batch from a table not in your subject area."

Mr. Ingles' table had traded with the English Department. "Hey," he said loudly, looking over the paper he had been handed, "somebody in English misspelled commitment in his marginal notes."

Dr. Miller interrupted the laughter almost before it started. It was getting late, and he still had quite a lot to do. "Okay. Since English seems to be considered so vulnerable, let's hear the spread of grades given on the essay question on *Macbeth*."

He asked for the hands of those people holding English papers. Then he asked for a show of hands from those people with English papers graded below 70 or *C*. Two went up. "What were the actual grades?"

"I have 68," one teacher said from the back of the room.

"This one has a large *C* with a small minus circled in blue ink. Maybe it means one is for content and one is for grammar."

"You get an *A*," someone from the English table quipped.

"Okay, hold on," Dr. Miller called for quiet. Then he asked for people with an English paper with an *A* or with 90 or more. Three hands went up.

"Aha! What did I tell you," Ingles said triumphantly. His smug assurance lit up his face.

"What are the actual grades and comments?" Dr. Miller asked.

" '*A*—Very thought-provoking!' "

" 'Couldn't agree with you less,' "came the second response, " 'but I admire the way you put it.' "

"I've got an even better one than that," said a third teacher, " '*A* and *B*+ equal *A*−.' "

"That's separate grading for grammar and content, then figured together," someone said stonily from the English Department. No one looked too happy in that Department now.

"Well," said Dr. Miller slowly, pacing back and forth

in front of the lectern, "who is right and who is wrong? Is it an *A* paper or a *C* paper? Or is it somewhere in between? And for that matter, what would have happened if you had known the student? And what if this were the 35th paper you had read at one sitting, instead of the first? And perhaps even more relevant, would the grade have been the same, say, if this were a Monday instead of a Friday? I wonder. . ."

"Very well, Dr. Miller," Ingles spoke out. He was no longer smiling. "You may be making some points where it concerns the English Department, but I'd like to see the spread among the science papers, if you don't mind."

The professor nodded. "Okay. That's a fair request. Let's do it with a show of hands. How many science papers were marked lower than *C*, 69 or under?" Two hands went up. "Between 70 and 79?" Two hands. "Over 90?" One hand.

"Why, that's ridiculous," Ingles shot up again. "I don't believe it. There are only seven of us in the Department and that paper deserved a solid *B*."

"You're crazy," Cliff Harper stood up and faced Ingles. "Just because the kid has the right answers doesn't mean he knows how he got them. Unless a student goes through the entire process, I take off points. Doesn't everybody?"

"I don't know about everybody," Ingles sputtered back, his face turning pink. "It's enough for me that they get the right answers. I always give different exams and seat kids alternately, so there is no cheating in my class. If they get the answer, by golly, they've solved the problem; and I'm not going to be bothered collecting scrap paper."

The debate between the two science teachers was drowned out by the hubbub of controversy erupting around the room. Dr. Miller allowed the teachers to argue among themselves a bit longer as he whispered something in Mr. Crewson's ear. Crewson nodded, then Dr. Miller walked back and slammed his fist on the table for quiet.

"Hold on now," he said. "It's quite obvious that grades mean different things to different people—even in the so-called objective disciplines like math and science. Now let's try one more experiment before we call it a day."

He didn't wait for comments. He asked the teachers to get out a piece of scrap paper and to put numbers on it from one to ten.

"This is a quiz," he said, "and may be used to determine your next salary increase. Or maybe we'll use your grade to decide who gets slow classes next year."

Ingles, along with a few other teachers, glared up at the professor. This time there was no laughter. Dr. Miller ignored the hostile faces and launched right into the questions ."Question one: What is a *standard deviation?*"

"You must be kidding," Miss Doyle said loudly.

He was not kidding. "Question two: Explain what a *mean* is. Three: Define *median*. Four: What is a *normal distribution?* Five: What is a *reliable test?"*

Ingles threw down his pencil. "This is ridiculous! What's he trying to do?" His face had now turned a glowing red.

Dr. Miller ignored the remark. He continued asking his questions in a cold and confident staccato. "What is *validity?* What is *objectivity?* List the measurements you use to determine the *reliability* of one of your own tests. How do you know that the last quiz you gave was *valid?"*

"And finally, tell me please . . . *what right do you have to grade other people's children?"*

The room was silent as Dr. Miller looked out across the lectern at the Mapleton High School faculty. Most of the teachers had stopped writing by question #4. No teacher would look back at Dr. Miller. Fingernails were being studied; desks and papers were under examination.

Looking out at those hiding faces, Dr. Miller sensed their anger and embarrassment. Finally, in a softer tone Dr. Miller said, "I suppose I should apologize for the harsh way I asked those last ten questions, but my own objectivity where grading is concerned is sometimes strained. You see, I believe that when we grade, we are using potentially very dangerous numbers. We need to be more careful. We need to know what we're doing, especially when the grades these days can determine who gets sent to Vietnam and who stays behind, or when our grading systematically screens out black kids from getting some of the benefits in this world of ours. The stakes are too high.

"Personally, and I know some of you will find my statement heretical, I seriously question the usefulness of traditional grading. I think there is nothing which more effectively separates students from teachers, which pits the educator and the learner against each other, when they should be working together. Each enemy is equipped with vicious weapons. The student has his crib sheets, his ponies, his apple-polishing, rote memorization, fawning obsequiousness, and other kinds of con-artistry. On our side, we teachers resort to mickey mouse assignments, surprise quizzes, unannounced notebook checks, tricky multiple-choice questions, and irrelevant essay questions—choose 3 out of 4. The worst thing we do, however, is set up a series of easily-graded hurdles which we mistake for learning. And we call ourselves teachers? Nonsense! We have allowed ourselves to become a group of overseers who drive the most reluctant group of field hands any plantation has ever known.

"I hope this is just the beginning of your search for some ways to change the grading system. From your sullen silence I can only guess that most of you don't know the first thing about standard deviation, reliability, validity and the rest; yet you continue to play the grading game. There's something *immoral* about that. There's something *immoral* about playing with kids' lives when you don't know which end of a bell-shaped curve is up." He started to gather his transparencies together.

"I think there are some serious problems here that you need to face. Looking at this print-out, I see a tremendous spread of opinion as to what things should be considered in grading. You have been so busy, for so many years, adding up your little numbers that you just aren't aware of how differently the teacher down the hall is looking at the same kids.

"But all of us continue to enter our letters of the alphabet and seem to have the blind faith that the people who use them are going to use them wisely. To be blunt, grades aren't *reliable* numbers or *valid* numbers or even *significant* numbers. Yet we continue to teach kids that they had better live and die on the little numbers we pass out every six or nine or fifteen weeks.

"Perhaps the worst thing is that you probably have a self-righteous streak which denies just how biased you are in your grading. Take question #7 from the series we ran through the computer. More than 90% of you said that social class should not be considered at all when grading; and yet, you are all aware that the students in the general sections of this high school are there because of their social class. You justify not putting them into college entrance sections on the grounds that they are too lazy or that they supposedly cannot read. Those general students have been neatly 'classed out' of the rewards of this school.

"Or take question #8: 'Should the student's ability to give you back exactly the same answers you want be considered in his grade?' Well, on your IBM cards you denied that this is a factor in your own grading. At least 83% of you said that it should not be given much weight, or definitely should not be considered when grading.

"However, I'm not sure your students believe that to be true of you. I have had a chance to interview hundreds of high school students in the context of a research study on student dissent I'm doing. It is shocking to see the unanimity students feel about even their best teachers' demanding certain exact answers and not settling for a point of view other than their own. Students are convinced that not giving the teacher what he wants to hear will lead to a lower grade. We've taught our students *that* notion, at least, very well."

Dr. Miller suddenly sounded weary. "I'll leave this print-out with Mr. Cunningham. I'm hoping he'll want to call another meeting about this topic in the near future. Thank you very much for your time and attention."

Dr. Miller sat down to mixed applause.

11 | *The Faculty Faces the Facts*

WITH HER FACE still stinging from the late January cold, Doris Doyle walked into school on Monday morning, entered the main office, said, "Hi, everyone," and walked over to the sign-in sheet. She signed her name on the sheet, checked the wall clock, and wrote in the correct time next to her name. Phil Dilling was staring at the Spanish teacher, Sally Keating, who was putting the finishing touches on a ditto master for her morning's lesson.

"Morning, Phil. How are things with you this morning?" Doris asked.

"Huh? What? Oh, it's you, Doris. Good morning."

"How did you like the meeting Friday, Phil?"

"Huh? Oh, well, I liked it all right."

Mr. Ingles abruptly set the ditto machine in neutral and said, "You didn't *believe* that professor, did you, Doris?"

"As a matter of fact, Charles, I think he was about the most refreshing thing to walk into school in a long time," she said.

Ken Harris, sitting by Mr. Cunningham's door, looked up over his *Daily News* and said, "You probably would enjoy any man walking into your life, Doris."

"All except you, tabloid. Hey, what did you think of what Dr. Miller said?"

Ken Harris, driver education instructor, assistant line coach and part-time guidance counselor in charge of college entrance, put down his newspaper and said, "I would say he had about as much reality as those mileage claims out of Detroit. He should visit the guidance office one of these days and see how we have to feed those colleges every grade-point average each kid has ever made from kindergarten right up. There's where grades have their moment of truth."

"I don't know what *you* mean by reality," Dilling remarked, "but I thought there was a new kind of reality I learned about Friday, with the grades on our science papers having the kind of spread they did. I thought for sure English would come off badly, but when *we* looked so bad, I really got disturbed."

"Ah, Dilling, that was sheer trickery. That particular paper was designed to give us a spread, and I think we are very naive to be taken in by his showmanship," Ingles said.

"I realize that you are an older, more experienced teacher, Mr. Ingles," Sally Keating said, "but I'm not sure you did very well on his last questions about mean, and deviation and those other statistical terms." Her voice was syrupy but with an edge of hostility in it.

"Now, now, Sally," Doris said, "none of us did very well on those damn questions; but that last one sent a chill through me. Just what right *do* I have to grade other people's children?"

"I never saw that grading business so clearly before," Sally admitted. "If that Dr. Miller was looking for a disciple, he's got one. I'm going to be talking about grading in each of my classes today. I'm going to ask my kids those same ten questions about grading that Dr. Miller asked us. I want to see what my students feel about the issues of feeding us what we want to hear, and what they think about the social class bias of grades. You know, I'm looking foward to this morning's classes more than I have since I began teaching. See you all later."

Charlie Ingles just shook his head.

"Go get 'em, Sally," Doris said encouragingly. "I think you've given me an idea which sure beats what I had planned for today: learning how to make lump-free gravy!"

"You'll both get your lumps," Ken Harris warned. "Ingles is right. Grades will be here long after both of you have retired to St. Petersburg to rock in the sun, because they're reality, ladies, *reality*."

"Well, Ken baby, reality has been known to change. And one of the ways I think I'm going to help is to turn my students on to a few of the things Dr. Miller said to us—good scholarly facts and academically respectable insights—and let reality fall where it may."

Later that afternoon, Biff Johnson, Robert Jeffreys, Walter Cannon and Cliff Harper were seated together at a table in the rear of the library, waiting for the regular Monday afternoon faculty meeting to begin.

From the bits and pieces they could hear of other conversations in the room, the faculty members were still expressing heated reactions to Friday's meeting. Although the four men had somewhat differing viewpoints on the grading issue, they all felt the subject was critically important.

"Did you see the look on those science teachers' faces when *their* grades on that paper were just about as varied as everyone else's?" Johnson remarked, and nudged Jeffreys so hard he almost dropped his cup of tea.

"I've only been here a semester," Jeffreys said, "but that was, without doubt, the most interesting faculty meeting we've had this year."

"You said it, brother," Harper agreed. "I asked MacIntyre to give that speech, not because I agreed with him—as a matter of fact, I didn't—but because I knew those kids would start thinking for a change. But after hearing Miller, I really have some doubts about grading. I don't think I'd go as far as you, though, Walt. I talked about a blanket *B* with my students, but the idea just didn't sit right with me. Anyway, I'm really interested in seeing how your brainstorm works out."

"You're no more curious than I, Cliff. The only difference I've been able to see so far is that the kids are a lot livelier and more interested in what they're doing. Oh, and I guess a lot more relaxed."

"Yeah, but that's just at the beginning, maybe," said Jeffreys. "After a while, when the novelty wears off, they may start to slough off."

"I guess it's a real possibility. But, then it becomes my problem to keep the class vital and interesting. We'll just have to see, and deal with the problem when the time comes, *if* it comes."

The library was rapidly filling with teachers, most of them heading directly to the coffee machine on the portable kitchen cart.

"Well, at least you're *doing* something, Walt," said his friend Harper. "I don't think I've done any big experiment like that since the year we both started here. Boy, do you remember how *that* one went?"

"Yes. But remember, that was your first year. I think if I had tried this blanket *B* my first year, I just wouldn't have had enough going for me in the class to pull it off."

"I sure know what you mean," said Jeffreys. "This first year has certainly been an up and down one for me. I'm glad, though, to be in a school that's willing to take an honest look at itself, like this one is."

"Us *honest?*" Biff questioned laughingly. "Do you actually *believe* there's a snowball's chance in hell of our taking this grading thing much further? My hunch is that we'll talk about it today, you know, tear down everything Miller said Friday, and then that will be that for the soul-searching at Mapleton High."

"I'm afraid Biff's right, Bob," Harper said. "You just watch how Cunningham tries to smooth things over if the discussion gets too lively. He's a good man, but he's up for an assistant superintendency one of these years, and I don't think he wants to make any more waves than he can help."

"At least you have to admit that he's allowed us free rein to explore the grading issue. He hasn't said anything about my kids' going around to different classes talking about their *Position Paper,* and he called that meeting Friday when he could have stalled us for a few more weeks. Sure, he's raised some questions with me about my grading system—but he hasn't told me what to do—and some of his questions were good ones."

"Better keep it down," Biff said. "Here he comes now. My only point was that he doesn't want to rock the boat. He doesn't care what you do with your classes as long as the kids do their work, their parents don't complain, and the faculty is one big, happy family."

Cunningham gave his teachers their usual ten minutes' leeway (which they had come to expect and were now trying to stretch to fifteen) and then began the meeting.

"As you know, we have the ten-year evaluation coming up next year, and we had wanted to plan our committees early so that we would be prepared when the time came. I see this as the major agenda item for this afternoon. Hopefully, we can all be out of here by 4:30."

The four teachers at the rear table looked at each other quizically, as did many others throughout the room.

"But before going into that, I though perhaps you'd like to spend a few minutes commenting on Friday's special meeting. I must say, judging from what I've heard, the reactions to Professor Miller's presentation were quite varied. Therefore, maybe we should get a sampling of these views before moving on. Who would like to start the ball rolling?"

He waited, looking with some discomfort around the room. Several teachers furtively avoided his glance, as students would do who had not done their homework and did not want to be called upon. Other teachers exchanged brief comments with their friends, but no one seemed willing to take the floor.

Finally Cunningham said, "Well, that's surprising. I thought perhaps you'd be interested in exploring this a bit. But if not, then I guess we can move along to . . . yes, Miss Keating?"

Sally, who had decided to try out Dr. Miller's grading experiment with her own classes, rose very nervously to speak. What she had to say would clearly have been difficult for any veteran faculty member, but for a new teacher, given the situation, it was even harder. She held her hands together to steady them.

"Well, Mr. Cunningham, I'm not exactly sure how many people in this room I speak for, but I think that many of us would very much like to discuss the issue of grades. I know the other language teachers and I have been discussing it quite a bit since the students brought it up and even more since Friday's meeting. I think we were expecting, well, hoping to spend the *whole* meeting today on the matter of grading."

She looked around to her colleagues for support. Finding many heads nodding their approval and relief, she continued.

"I know I've just started to become concerned with this issue, and I'm just beginning to realize how many unanswered questions I have about grades. And I don't think I'm the only one."

Several voices, addressed to her but clearly aimed at Cunningham, echoed, "Here, here;" "That's right;" "Good point;" and "You're *not* the only one." Miss Keating sat down.

"She's right, Joe," Ingles remarked. "We've *got* to talk about this thing. There are a lot of notions going around about grading that need investigation. I, for one, have heard a lot of ideas that seem way off base to me, and I'd sure like to get the chance to say publicly what I think about them."

"Yes, Charley, I'm sure that *would* be valuable. My only concern is one of time. You know, we have just so many faculty meetings in a year, and we do have this evaluation coming up . . ."

Biff Johnson broke in. "Oh, hell, Joe. That evaluation's a year away. What in heaven's name is this grading issue if not a *self*-evaluation? So why don't we get on with it?"

Many heads and voices indicated their support of Johnson's statement. It was clear to everyone, including Cunningham, which way the wind was blowing.

"Well, if most of you feel this way, I certainly have no objection. Very well, who has something to say on Dr.

Miller's speech or on the subject of grading in general?"

The first few comments were gentle, middle-of-the-road statements. Dr. Miller had some good points, but perhaps he had exaggerated; many of the students against grading were probably sincerely motivated, but many were just along for the ride and the hope of getting out of some work; the teachers should read more about the subject; and so on.

"You know," said Alf Bronson, "I've been sitting here listening to you people talk about this as if this were a philosophical issue. This isn't *philosophy* we're dealing with; this is *reality!* We've got a hundred kids running all over this building doing a pretty good job of convincing the rest of the student body that grading is everything from immoral to illegal. And now, although we've never discussed the matter openly, we've got about five teachers in the school who have decided to conduct their own experiments with different kinds of grading. Now it . . ."

Cunningham interrupted him, "Excuse me. I'd just like to add that I've got more and more parents calling me every day, concerned and annoyed about what's going on here. That's all. Sorry for interrupting."

"OK, there you are," Bronson continued. "This is a real issue we've got to deal with. These kids aren't playing games; for better or worse, they're serious. So I think we should stop talking about this as though it's an abstract issue which doesn't have anything to do with us. The question is not only what we *think* of grading, but what do we plan to *do* about it at Mapleton High School? I don't know what I think about that myself, but I *do* know we've got to decide. Are we going to change anything about our grading system, or are we going to do exactly as we've always done? If it's the latter, why don't we tell the kids now and save them a lot of trouble?"

Bronson's speech changed the tone. The discussion became more serious, more real. They discussed grades and motivation, grades and competition, grades and college, grades and values, grades and objectivity, grades and the teacher-student relationship, grades and cheating.

The discussion, although lively and often heated, went round and round and arrived nowhere. Near 5:30, when several teachers began to act upon their frustration and make movements toward leaving, Cunningham took over.

"Well, it seems people's stamina has just about given out this afternoon. I know it's been a long day, and I'm sorry to have kept you this late, but I must say it has been valuable."

Biff Johnson was angry. "No, it *hasn't* been valuable, Joe. We've talked all afternoon, and we haven't made one decision. We've been arguing about Miller's presentation, but we don't know whether *our own* opinions are based on facts or a lot of hot air. We've been talking about alternatives to the grading system, yet we don't even know which alternatives are available to us. I know it's late, but let's not leave before *something concrete* comes out of this meeting."

Enough applause greeted Johnson's plea that Cunningham had to respond.

"OK, Biff, that's a good point. If I understand you, you're saying that we need to know more about the grading system. Does it work? Can it be effective? Can we make it more effective? What do grades tell us? Is what Dr. Miller said on Friday true? In other words, what does the *research* say about the subject? What knowledge exists in the books that can help us answer these questions?

"There's a PTA meeting about three weeks from today. I have a friend who is a professor at Central State —he was originally supposed to come last Friday, but he couldn't make it, so Miller came in his place. Why don't I ask my friend to come to the PTA meeting and tell all of us, parents and teachers alike, what the research says on the subject of grading. Instead of our having a regular faculty meeting that week, we'll attend the PTA meeting and find out what we need to know about grading. The meeting will also be informative for the parents and other members of the community. I'm sure this friend of mine will present a much broader, more objective and less emotionally-charged presentation. What do you think?"

Everyone liked the idea, but Walter Cannon wanted to go even further.

"Joe, I like your idea, and it's great if we can kill two

birds with one stone: present some of the facts about grading to both teachers and parents. But I'm afraid there's a third bird that needs killing. If we're really serious about finding out all we can about grading and whether or not we have the best possible grading system at Mapleton High, I think we have to find out what the other alternatives are which are open to us. We all know there's a lot of experimentation with grading across the country. I'd like to propose that we form a faculty committee, with some students on it as well, to explore alternative grading systems for Mapleton High. After the alternatives have been evaluated, the committee would report their findings to the whole faculty. We would then be in a much better position to discuss this issue intelligently."

"Well, Walter," Cunningham said, "that certainly seems like a sound idea. What does concern me is that the project you propose would take a lot of work. We don't have the money to pay faculty members any extra. I'd feel very uncomfortable asking any faculty member to . . ."

"Don't be silly, Joe," Doris said. "I'd like to volunteer to be on the committee."

"So would I," Walter stated. "I know some of my students will want to help with the work also."

"I guess I'd like to join that gruesome two-some," Cliff Harper said. "I'm not sure where I stand on this issue, but I'm becoming more and more interested. This will be a good way for me to learn some facts about grading."

"Well, it looks like you're going to have a committee after all," Cunningham said. "But I think if this committee is going to represent the faculty, it should represent all views, if you know what I mean . . ."

"OK, Joe, I get the hint," Russ Collins conceded. "I'm not exactly a radical when it comes to the subject of grading, so I guess I'll balance out this committee."

"Thank you, Russ," Cunningham said. "If there is any way the office can help any of you, just let me know.

"So, I guess that's it for today. I'll put out a reminder about the PTA meeting, and I'm sure the Committee on Alternatives will keep us informed of its progress. We'll see you tomorrow morning. Meeting dismissed."

The teachers left the library and walked out to the darkened parking lot. As Biff Johnson walked toward his car, he yelled back to Jeffreys, "You'll see I'm right, kid. Not a snowball's chance in hell!"

12 | *The PTA Hears about the Research on Grades*

THE PTA MEETING took place as planned, in the school cafeteria. Professor Robert Standish of Central State College was the guest speaker. Two hundred and six parents were present, as well as fifty-eight teachers— an unusually large turn-out.

Cunningham had asked the boys from audio-visual to tape-record the meeting. Later he had transcripts of the entire meeting printed and distributed to all the teachers and members of the PTA. The following is a portion of the transcript:

Since so many are here on such a cold and forbidding evening, this grading business has obviously kindled your interest. I'm pleased to be in a position to help clarify the issues. Actually, I personally lived with grades for nearly thirty years, as a student and then as a teacher, without once seriously questioning their presence. In the past five months, however, my own research has changed all that; and I am not only interested, but, as your children would say, I've been 'turned on.' I'm not going to be too technical and bore you with a lot of figures and statistics, although occasionally I will refer to a study of particular relevance. Mainly, I see this as your evening to air the questions on your minds concerning this very crucial issue. In case some of you wish to pursue a particular question at greater length, I will leave some copies of my annotated bibliography. Please feel free to take one after the meeting [See: Appendix I]. Now, let's begin with your questions. . . . Yes, sir?

WELL, SIR, UH, DOCTOR, WHEN I LOOK BACK AT THE OLDEN DAYS WHEN I ATTENDED SCHOOL, I REALLY WORKED HARD FOR GRADES. NOW, WHEN I SEE MY OWN CHILD AT HOME AND KNOW WHAT PRESSURE I HAVE TO APPLY TO GET HIM TO DO HIS HOMEWORK, I'M FRIGHTENED TO THINK HOW LITTLE HE MIGHT DO WITHOUT THE GRADING TO GIVE HIM THE INCENTIVE.

Actually, this *is* a very common fear. But, perhaps the concern is misdirected. We should really be worrying about whether our children can only be motivated by the use of grades rather than by *interest* in the subject matter. In any case, your question is: do grades actually motivate students? To this question, I have to answer both yes and no.

There *are* certain students who are motivated by grades (33, 50, 51)*—interestingly enough, usually the better students who need motivation the least. They have been encouraged to do well in school and *have* done well.

---

* Numbers in parentheses refer to specific research reports in the Annotated Bibliography which refer to studies directly applicable to the question under consideration.

As a result, schoolwork comes more easily, and they find it more interesting. Grades for them are rewards.

But what about the other kids: the ones who have trouble with schoolwork and who do *not* do well? I'm afraid that grades have just the opposite effect. These are the students who need success and encouragement the most. Lack of success in a competitive, grade-oriented system does not generate higher levels of aspiration or expectations of excellence (1, 33, 36, 51, 53). Instead, their failures destroy what little motivation they have. So, one way to look at motivation is to say that those who need motivation the least are most motivated by grades; those who need motivation the most tend to be turned off by grades.

Sir, does this answer your question?

YES, THANK YOU.

Actually, there's another way to look at this question of motivation. We usually think of motivation in the *short* run. "If grading weren't involved, I wouldn't do my homework." "Boy, if I didn't have to worry about grades, I'd sure goof off." I'm sure most of us have heard these statements or variations of them, or even expressed these feelings ourselves.

But can you envision, for a moment, living year after year under an educational system without grades? Let your imagination loose a bit. OK, maybe for a while you'd take it easy; you'd cut corners in the subjects you didn't like. But isn't it possible that after a while your *as grades have ... taken ... within ... year ... way can't we grade?*

own interest in learning would begin to motivate you to work? Isn't it possible that after a period of time you'd begin to throw yourself into your work and accomplish even *more,* based on *your own* motivation (we educational psychologists call it "intrinsic motivation"), than you would operating under the extrinsic motivation of grades?

Maybe this sounds a little far-fetched to you, or too idealistic, but I'd like to tell you about a study I consider the most profoundly important research study ever undertaken in the history of American education. It's called the "Eight-Year Study" (78). The results were first published in 1942 when the country was at war; perhaps this is why the results seem to have been lost on most educators.

The aim of the experiment was to determine just how important a rigid college-oriented curriculum, including grades, was to a student's later success in college. During a period of eight years, a research team took more than 1,500 students from 30 high schools and matched them with an equal number of other students. Thus, *every* student in one group was paired with another student who, as much as was humanly possible, was similar in terms of such variables as age, sex, religion, socio-economic background, parent income, grade average, subjects taken and areas of special interest.

One group of schools—the experimental group—was allowed almost a free hand in determining how they would develop their high school program in preparation for college. Many of them eliminated grading. Three hundred cooperating colleges agreed to accept students from these schools, based on the principal's recommendation. The other group—the control group—went through the typical, graded program. What do you think the results were?

In *every* aspect of college life—grades earned, campus leadership positions attained, drop-out rate, extra-curricular participation, and so on—the experimental group did *just as well as or slightly better than* the traditionally-graded and traditionally-educated students. In fact, the experimental group earned slightly higher grades in college, were judged to be more resourceful and more intellectually curious, and were perceived as more objective in their thinking than the control group.

This study was conducted with extreme care; but this *was* only *one* study which no one has ever been able to duplicate. Nevertheless, the traditional grading system has never been shown to be the most effective way of motivating students to work.

Yes, another question?

DR. STANDISH, WE HAVE THREE CHILDREN IN SCHOOL—TWO IN HIGH SCHOOL. I NEVER WENT TO COLLEGE, BUT IT'S ALWAYS BEEN MY UNDERSTANDING THAT YOU SIMPLY CANNOT GET INTO COLLEGE WITHOUT GRADES, AND GOOD ONES AT THAT. SO AREN'T GOOD GRADES NECESSARY, AND AREN'T THEY GOING TO BE USED BY THE COLLEGES TO PREDICT WHETHER OUR CHILDREN CAN

Well, sir, I hear two questions there. One is whether your children need good grades or not. That's an easy one. As long as this school gives traditional grades, then if your child wants to go to a college that wants high grades, he'd better have them. I guess that's pretty obvious.

But the other question you raise is a little more complicated. You imply that the reason colleges want grades is because they are good predictors of whether or not a candidate for admission will succeed in that college.

In one sense, that's true. Past grades do predict future grades with considerable accuracy. Thus, if a student has high grades in elementary school, there is some assurance that he will maintain these in high school (62, 63, 64, 67, 69). However, the higher up the educational ladder he climbs, the less true this is. Thus, predicting success in graduate school from grades in college is much more difficult than predicting success in college from high school grades (67, 75).

Nevertheless, although high school grades *are* the best *single* predictor for success in college, they are still *poor* predictors (88). High school grades still represent only a *small part* of all the factors or ingredients which go into determining how successful a student will be in college. Let's look at it this way. If we were to take a large pot and fill it to the top with all the ingredients necessary to predict, with absolute certainty, an individual's future academic success, putting only grades into the pot would still leave the pot two-thirds *empty*. A wide variety of other variables or ingredients must be added, such as support from the home, interest in the particular course of studies, maturity factors, boy-friend or girl-friend problems, physical or emotional problems, the kinds of teachers encountered, holding an outside job, and so on. The list can go on until the pot is slowly filled to the top.

Now, why do I tell you all this? For the simple reason that nearly half of the students who enter a state university *do not graduate* from that institution. Many of them are unable to make the academic grade. Thus, many universities and colleges are beginning to realize that the present system of screening applicants—a system which places great emphasis on grades—is turning out to be an enormous financial and intellectual waste. A study at the University of Michigan (48) indicated that it is more practical, from a financial point of view, to study each applicant for admissions individually rather than using more gross screening procedures, such as the grade-point average and high school rank. Success is dependent on too many non-intellectual factors. Perhaps this example will prove to be a trend that will be beneficial to your children and mine when they face the selection process.

I believe a gentleman in the third row had a question.

THANK YOU. IN SPITE OF WHAT YOU JUST SAID, IT SEEMS

TO ME THAT IT SHOULD BE VERY IMPORTANT FOR A STU-
DENT TO OBTAIN GOOD GRADES IN SCHOOL SINCE, AFTER
ALL, THE CLASSROOM IS AN ATTEMPT TO CREATE A SLICE
OF REAL LIFE, AND ONE MUST BE ABLE TO ADAPT TO COM-
PETITION IN OUR SOCIETY. SO WHY NOT BEGIN IN
SCHOOL AND GET ALL THE PRACTICE ONE CAN? I'M SURE
HOW WELL ONE DOES IN BUSINESS . . . OUT IN REAL
LIFE . . . CAN BE PREDICTED FROM GRADES.

I realize that what I am going to tell you now will
be difficult for you to accept, but here goes. *There has
been shown to be virtually no relationship between success in work and the grades received by those people
entering a particular occupational field* (61, 66, 71).
Thus, strange as it may seem, grades in teacher education courses have no relationship to successful teaching.
In other words, what it takes to be a good teacher has
very little to do with what it takes to be a good student
in teacher education courses (56, 57, 59). Nor do
grades received in medical school predict who will be
the most successful medical practitioners (72). Even
in a field as technical as engineering, those recognized
as most competent in the field could not be predicted
from their previous school grades (70). In addition
to these facts, educational programs outside our public
schools and universities seldom use grades as a means
of reporting performance. Industry, a huge trainer of
manpower, evaluates its management trainees and em-
ployees-on-the-job by means of accomplishment, usually
based on behavioral measures which are translated in

the form of detailed reports rather than grades. Not only are grades apparently poor predictors of on-the-job performance, but people out on the job don't even use them in *their own* evaluations.

I believe there was a question in the back row.

DOCTOR, WE HAVE A STUDENT AT HOME WHO ISN'T GETTING VERY GOOD GRADES, AT LEAST NOT AS GOOD AS THEY SHOULD BE. HE REPORTS TO US THAT ONE OF THE MAIN REASONS IS THAT THERE IS A LOT OF CHEATING GOING ON IN SCHOOL—NOT ONLY IN TESTS AND QUIZZES, BUT ON ALL KINDS OF PAPERS AND HOMEWORK ASSIGNMENTS. HE SAYS HE TRIES TO DO HIS OWN WORK, AND THIS CREATES MANY PROBLEMS FOR HIM. I KNOW HE'S TRYING TO PASS THE BUCK A BIT, BUT IT DOES MAKE ME QUESTION WHAT IS GOING ON AND WHETHER THERE IS ANYTHING THAT CAN BE DONE ABOUT IT.

That's an easy one to answer. In the research, there is considerable evidence to suggest that cheating is not only a common fact of life, but is apparently accepted by most students. If you ask one hundred students if they have cheated, chances are that between 50% and 80% will say "yes;" and the majority of these will admit to having cheated during the last term (29, 35, 41, 76, 88). A large number will admit to cheating regularly. Although honor systems somewhat reduce cheating, I'm sorry to say that cheating will exist as long as it pays; and in our present grading system, apparently cheating pays well.

Could I have another question please?

AS YOU SAY, MOST STUDENTS CHEAT AT ONE TIME OR
ANOTHER. STILL, IN SPITE OF THE PROBLEMS WITH
GRADES, I'M A TRUE BELIEVER IN THE IDEA THAT THE
CREAM WILL ALWAYS RISE TO THE TOP, AND THIS HAP-
PENS, AS WELL, IN THE GRADING SYSTEM.

There is no doubt in my mind that many good students will survive in spite of the system. However, I'm
interested in ways to bring out the most potential from
each individual. Not long ago a research team gave
an intelligence test to all of the children in four elementary schools (14). The teachers were told that the
tests were given to reveal which students would probably show the greatest gain in IQ during the rest of the
school year. This seed was purposely planted in the
minds of the teachers.

Ten students were selected at random from each of
the participating classes, and the teachers were told
that *these children* were the ones who would show the
most improvement in IQ during the year. Well, at the
end of the year all of the students were given another
IQ test. And, you guessed it, *the students who had been
selected at random* in the kindergarten, first, second and
third grades of these four schools showed *significantly
greater gains in IQ* than did the other students. Obviously, since the teachers *thought* these students were

special, they must have given them more attention and reinforcement during the year than they did the other students. Not only were the teachers' opinions influenced by the first test, but their behaviors were also influenced. The "selected" students were no different from the rest of the students in the four schools, but because they were treated with favor, they responded to the learning situation in a more positive manner. They even ranked higher in such areas as cooperativeness, interest and social adjustment.

If this one test condition can so drastically alter the learning for the selected students, one wonders what subtle conditions are constantly at work in the classroom which influence the grades a student will eventually get. Who knows what forces the "cream" to rise to the surface in a class and what keeps it from happening. A look at last year's report card, a rumor from a previous teacher, the clothes a child wears, his language, skin color or parents? A grading system seems to maximize the impact of these subjective variables rather than striving to reduce them as much as possible. Yes, some of the cream does get to the top, *in spite of* our grading system; but much too much becomes sour and gets wasted.

PROFESSOR, ALL OF THIS IS VERY INTERESTING, BUT I FIND IT ABSOLUTELY ESSENTIAL THAT MY CHILD BRING HOME REPORT CARD GRADES. THIS IS THE ONE SURE WAY I HAVE OF TELLING JUST HOW WELL SHE IS DOING IN

RELATION TO OTHER STUDENTS IN HER CLASS. I'M SURE OTHER PARENTS HERE WOULD AGREE WITH ME.

I can readily understand your concern. As a parent, you would like to know how your child is doing in school. The problem with the report card is that it tells you next to nothing about what you really *should* want to know. Does it tell you what your son's or daughter's strengths are? Does it indicate his or her weaknesses? Does it make recommendations for improvement? Does it suggest what you, as a parent, might do to help?

NO, BUT AT LEAST IT TELLS ME HOW MY DAUGHTER IS DOING—WHETHER SHE'S JUST GETTING BY OR WHETHER SHE'S DOING GOOD WORK.

Well, sir, I wish I could agree with you there, but, unfortunately, I can't. Let's say, for example, that your daughter gets a *B* on her report card. You look at the key and you see that a *B* indicates "good" work. But let me ask you—"good" in respect to what? A *B* in one class might mean that the teacher has set standards for excellence and your daughter is almost achieving those standards (80). But in another class, she might be doing only "fair" work, in terms of her own capabilities, but "good" work compared to the rest of the class. So the teacher gives her a *B*. So the value of a given grade depends on the individual standards of that particular teacher. Now, the problem for the parent or the child is to figure out which line of thinking the teacher is taking. Unless you know the teacher's standards, the grade tells you very little.

Also, to understand a grade, the student or parent needs to determine whether the teacher uses a specific *curving method* as a means of categorizing students according to certain grades. What percentage of *A*'s, *B*'s, *C*'s, *D*'s or *F*'s a teacher is willing to allocate to any particular class is usually a well-kept secret by that teacher. For example, a teacher may believe that it is unreasonable to give more than 15% of the students *A*'s if the class is representative of a general population. Similarly, the teacher might expect that 15% of the group should probably fail. The largest number of students would naturally fall in the broad middle range represented by the *C* grade. Even if teachers don't admit to using a curve, studies of grading patterns suggest that teachers do have them in mind. They usually are not supported by any rationale other than whim. One major argument against this practice is that the aim of education is to establish reasonable objectives that are within the grasp of most students. So, hopefully, every student will do well, and there will be no need to give a prescribed percentage of low grades. Also, every class will naturally differ in terms of over all performance levels. Pre-established curves strike at the heart of individualized instruction (13, 25, 17, 81).

No, sir. Not in my experience anyway. First of all, I think it's a rare teacher who has carefully worked out *his own* grading standards and made these explicit to the students. But even where you do have teachers who have carefully worked out their own standards, you're not very likely to get very many of them to agree with one another.

There's some interesting information from a number of large universities which deals with this question directly and seems to be just as appropriate to high schools (11, 21, 22). The evidence is that if you have thirty instructors teaching thirty sections of the same course, with similar teaching objectives and a cross-sectional group of students, *the grading distribution will vary dramatically among the various instructors.* Thus, if Bill, by chance, gets instructor "X," he may find that 20% of the students flunk, 15% get *D*'s, 45% receive *C*'s, 15% have *B*'s and only 5% get *A*'s. But, by the luck of the draw, Tom gets instructor "Y" who is much more lenient and gives 30% *A*'s, 30% *B*'s, 35% *C*'s and only 5% *D*'s and does not flunk any student. The same course objectives, same basic materials, same general level of student ability. The primary difference? The instructors' views of "standards." Such huge discrepancies are common and may be found among instructors in the same departments, between departments and between different colleges. I have little doubt that the same problems arise whenever more than one teacher teaches the same course. The real pain comes when the *F* given by teacher "X" is the grade that drops the student two percentage points below the arbitrarily-established university expulsion cutoff point. Suddenly, what has been a *relative* measure of student performance becomes an *absolute* to be used with power and decisiveness in a decision-making process that may have lasting repercussions on the life of a particular student (73).

WELL, DR. STANDISH, IF GRADES VARY THIS MUCH WITHIN A DEPARTMENT OR A SCHOOL, I'D HATE TO THINK HOW MUCH THEY VARY BETWEEN SCHOOLS. IS THIS TRUE?

Ironically, no; but now we do run into a different problem. Although schools differ greatly in what they teach, how they teach and how their students perform, their grading patterns are amazingly similar. Thus, the distribution of *A*'s at a school like Harvard will not be very different from that of the most mediocre colleges. If we can generalize this to high schools, it means that college entrance officers must make many subjective judgments to determine what the different grades mean from the enormous range of high schools who send them applicants. Suddenly *the argument as to why the university needs grades* to determine the applicant's abilities *loses some weight.*

But the same problems can be seen much closer to home. For example, a parent of a child in an inner-city school reads with mixed horror and anger that the children in his son's school are reading on an average of 2½ years below the national average. Yet, all along his son has been receiving *C*'s in reading. Average, but certainly passing . . . or so he thought. Or the straight-*A* student from Prankville, who has worked for four years in high school so she would be accepted at a fine eastern women's college, fails to be accepted because her "grades" are not competitive with those of better high schools.

I don't think we've heard from any teachers this evening. Do you have any questions or feelings you'd like to air?

YES, I DO! I'VE BEEN SITTING HERE FOR ALMOST AN HOUR, AND I FIND MYSELF BECOMING INCREASINGLY IRATE. MAYBE I SHOULDN'T FEEL PERSONALLY ATTACKED BY WHAT YOU'RE SAYING, BUT I DO. FIRST YOU INDICATE A FEW DOZEN TIMES HOW BIASED WE ARE, THEN YOU JUMP ON OUR STANDARDS. AND NOW, I SUPPOSE YOU BELIEVE THAT OUR TEACHERS, AFTER YEARS OF TRAINING AND AFTER DEVELOPING AT LEAST SOME DEGREE OF EXPERTISE . . . NOT TO MENTION MORAL RESPONSIBILITY TO OUR STUDENTS . . . I SUPPOSE WE ARE TO BELIEVE

THAT WE ARE NOT FAIR WHEN EVALUATING OUR STU-
DENTS.

In no way do I wish to build an attack on teachers.
I'm a teacher and am just as fallible as any of you.
Also, like you, I am a victim of the system. The issue
has nothing at all to do with moral responsibility. It
does have something to say about what I am capable
of, both good and bad, because I am *human*. Whatever
happens, I want to be aware of my limitations as an
evaluator of other people and try my best to be as fair
and helpful as possible. So, with that in mind, let me
give you some information about teacher grading that
we have known for at least sixty years and has been
thoroughly researched (10, 12, 18, 19, 20, 23).

If, for example, I were to give the same test paper to
100 teachers who teach the same subject and have
roughly equivalent training and levels of expertise, and
I were to ask them to grade the paper, let's say an English theme, on the basis of 100 points, with 75 being a
passing mark, do you know what we'd find? Almost certainly a range of grades from *D*'s and *F*'s in the 60's and
70's to *A*'s and *B*'s in the 80's and 90's (18). One study
(10) discovered nearly fifty different criteria teachers
used in grading, including everything from strictly measurable items like punctuation, spelling and sentence
structure, to less measurable content variables such as
theme, organization and style, to variables that are just
not measurable by any standards now used by teachers,

such as effort and creativity. Add to this the kinds of bias factors we've already talked about, as well as such variables as fatigue and general health (8), and it's little wonder that grading is *not* a very reliable art. The problem in a nutshell is that there are just too many influences impinging on the teacher to hope for equivalent standards. The same points hold true for math and science and all other subjects, as well as English (19). . .

BUT THAT'S HARD TO BELIEVE. A TRIANGLE IS A TRIANGLE IS A TRIANGLE. HOW COULD THERE BE VARIATION WHEN GRADING A MATH PAPER?

Well, it was discovered that some teachers have a thing about neatness, while others couldn't care less. Others were found to give partial credit if an answer were partly correct. Still others would accept nothing less than perfection. And, of course, some teachers made mistakes in their own calculations. It's even been found that *when you give teachers very specific criteria to guide their grading, they still produce a wide range of scores* (8).

One final point on this subject. So far we've been talking about varying standards among different teachers. Even more shattering to one's "grading image" is the fact that if you return a set of exams to a teacher, let's say two months after he first graded them, and ask him to grade them again, there is a good chance that every paper will have a different numerical mark, and the difference between marks on the first and the second papers will seldom be less than ten points (23). If you were to translate the numbers into letter grades, many of the grades might differ by one or two whole letters.

BUT IF THIS IS TRUE, HOW CAN A REPORT CARD EVEN SUGGEST THAT AN *A* GRADE REPRESENTS FROM 90 TO 100 POINTS, AND A *B* GRADE REPRESENTS FROM 80 TO 89 POINTS, AND SO ON? IF GRADING IS THAT VULNERABLE TO TEACHER WHIM AND INACCURACIES, THIS KIND OF GRADING WOULD BE TOTALLY UNFAIR TO BOTH THE TEACHER AND THE CHILD.

I believe you are probably right. It seems ludicrous to me that I am expected to categorize students into discrete grading boxes—either by number or letter—when I know just how difficult it is to measure performance accurately.

BUT, PROFESSOR STANDISH, ISN'T THIS WHY THE OBJECTIVE TESTS WERE DEVELOPED? YOU KNOW, THOSE WITH MULTIPLE CHOICE, FILL IN THE BLANK OR TRUE-FALSE QUESTIONS. AFTER WHAT YOU HAVE SAID ABOUT GRADING, THESE WOULD SEEM TO BE THE ONLY SOLUTION.

Perhaps so, but even with these tests there are inequities that must be taken into account and, all too often, are not (15). In the first place, developing a valid and reliable objective test requires an enormous amount of time on the part of the teacher. Remember, every question on such a test is selected in a subjective fashion by a teacher with certain pet interests. Secondly, once the scores are in, the teacher must still place a grade on the paper and decide how many correct responses earn an *A,* and so forth. Thirdly, the teacher determines whether the test will be one which measures how much a student knows, or one of those familiar guessing games designed to reveal how much the child does not know. A fourth point is that such tests often penalize those individuals who have done extra, outside reading. Trapped by this additional knowledge, they have more alternatives from which to choose when filling in the blank or deciding upon correct multiple-choice answers. A lot of knowledge *can,* in this case, be a dangerous thing. Finally, these tests may well lead students into a kind of short answer mentality. The thinking processes develop a sort of rigor mortis because only the memorization of certain specific facts and figures is necessary. I have had students enter the University who swear they had not written more than four or five essay papers or examinations during their four years in high school.

One point should be made quite clear. I'm all for a useful process of student evaluation which helps them understand their present level of academic performance in terms of specific course objectives. However, I am attempting to share with you the problems and inequities we introduce when we try to place the student's performance into discrete grade categories and then call this evaluation. Even though much of the information we have been examining tonight might be distressing to you, the research does shed light on some rather specific areas where things can be improved for you, the parents and the teachers, but most importantly, for the children who carry the burden of grades.

I believe there is still time for a few more questions. Let's try another from a teacher. Yes?

WE'VE BEEN TALKING A LOT ABOUT TEACHERS' BIASES AND THEIR INABILITY TO GIVE REALLY OBJECTIVE GRADES. I'M CURIOUS ABOUT A RELATED AREA AND PERHAPS YOU CAN HELP. I BELIEVE THAT WOMEN ARE OLD SOFT-SOAPS IN GRADING AND THAT THEY ARE ESPECIALLY LENIENT WITH GIRLS. THEY TELL ME THIS IS NONSENSE, AND THAT IT IS WE MEN WHO ARE REALLY BIASED IN FAVOR OF ANY SMILING OR TEARFUL GIRL WHO COMES OUR WAY. IS THERE ANY RESEARCH ON THIS?

It is difficult to say with any certainty whether women or men are more lenient in their grading. The evidence is just too inconclusive. But, I can say with great certainty that the female student is generally the recipient of higher grades than the male, even when the same levels of achievement have been shown (31, 32, 34, 43, 46). For example, in one experiment, approximately 400 boys and girls in grades 2 to 6 were given Achievement Tests. Contrary to expectations, the boys scored 8%

higher than the girls. But the comparison of *grades* between the boys and girls revealed that the girls averaged 8% higher than the boys. A likely conclusion is that the female students show a greater tendency to internalize the values of good conduct and conformity within the school environment than do the boys. These and other factors are seen as an implicit part of the grading process. Achievement is difficult enough to measure, but imagine how the grading equation is muddied when we begin adding neatness, troublesomeness, enthusiasm for the subject or noise level. Whatever the non-achievement variables, they *are* present and do influence the process of grade distribution (43).

The gentleman in the first row.

THIS LAST STUDY SUGGESTS A GREAT DEAL ABOUT WHAT IT TAKES TO BE SUCCESSFUL IN SCHOOL. I GUESS I'D LIKE TO KNOW IF THERE ARE ANY MEASURABLE DIFFERENCES THAT HAVE BEEN FOUND—OTHER THAN INTELLIGENCE—BETWEEN STUDENTS WHO GET HIGH GRADES IN SCHOOL AND THOSE WHO DON'T. AS YOU PUT IT, DOES A CERTAIN TYPE OF PERSON PLAY THE "GAME" BETTER THAN ANOTHER?

Well, first of all, students who are most liked by their teachers seem to perform better academically (36, 54). Those who tend to isolate themselves from the teacher, who are less willing to adopt the values of the school and who appear less satisfied, achieve at a lower level. Similarly, while there is some difference of opinion in the research (36, 52), good students tend to seek each other out, while students who feel alienated from school cluster together in friendship groups. One would think that this would lead to a reinforcement of certain values and behaviors which would further insure acceptance or rejection in the academic setting.

Students recognized as the high achievers appear less willing to take risks, are less dominating, more subject to group pressures and more persistent than those students who are less successful, but who may be as intelligent (38, 46). For students the grade is the focal point of the educational reward system. The good student will find out what the expectations are for receiving good grades and will tend to conform, whether the expectations are directly applicable to the learning process or not.

One study (28) found that students who responded to certain questions on an examination in accordance with the teacher's viewpoint and then received a high grade had a definite tendency to change their own original beliefs in the direction of the rewarded response. In contrast, students who received low grades for views which were divergent from those of the teacher tended to hold onto their own beliefs with greater tenacity. Thus, this information seems to suggest that there are measurable differences between achievers and non-achievers in terms other than intelligence.

WAD-JA-GET?

DR. STANDISH, IF GRADES PLAY SUCH A LARGE PART IN THE LIFE OF A SCHOOL, ONE WOULD EXPECT TO FIND OTHER REPERCUSSIONS, PERHAPS PSYCHOLOGICAL. IS THERE ANYTHING YOU CAN SAY LONG THIS LINE?

Students, like adults, try to find ways to protect themselves when a situation seems threatening. We tend to freeze, run away or play a role when faced with a threatening situation. Similarly, certain patterns of behavior will become evident when a group attempts to maintain its equilibrium and feeling of security.

In the face of the ever-present teacher evaluation and student competition, a continual source of tension and stress exists in school. Children cope with this condition by establishing certain group rules or norms, thus insuring some degree of safety for themselves. To be cooperative with the teacher, to show too much enthusiasm, to do extra work, to talk to the teacher after class: these are all considered taboo by the class (45). Most students would really like to get to know the teacher better, would like to show more interest and be more responsive and would like to do additional work if the subject interested them, but they refuse to transgress the established rules of conduct. If students weren't so fearful of adverse evaluation by the teacher, these rules would hardly be necessary; and the students would be able to learn in a more intellectually and emotionally honest environment.

BUT, DOESN'T ABILITY GROUPING CERTAINLY EQUALIZE SOME OF THE ACADEMIC PRESSURES?

Ability grouping does separate the achiever from the non-achiever. But there is no evidence to suggest that such segregation by classes (here I am not talking about special sections within a class for reading, math, etc.) has had a positive impact upon either the low- or high-achiever group (37). This process does, however, certainly determine lines of social relationships, leading to what can be called "selective deprivation" since it isolates important groups of students from each other. If there are no proven academic benefits from this kind of segregation, I wonder what good it does except to enhance the ego of the parents in what might be called the "elite" classes.

We only have time for one more question. Yes?

WELL, SIR, IF I MAY SAY SO, YOU'VE MADE A PRETTY DAMNING CASE AGAINST GRADING. IF GRADING MAKES AS LITTLE SENSE AS YOU'VE INDICATED, WHY HAS IT BEEN WITH US SO LONG? SECONDLY, IS THERE ANYTHING ANYBODY IS DOING TO FIND A BETTER METHOD OF GRADING? THIRDLY, WHAT WOULD YOU RECOMMEND FOR MAPLETON HIGH SCHOOL?

For a last question, you sure picked a winner! Briefly, the history and the research on grading indicate there isn't much substantial educational basis for grading.

Add to this the realization by many teachers that grading often complicates and interferes with classroom learning.

Although more individualized evaluation procedures might make greater sense, educationally speaking, they are more time-consuming for the teacher and costly for the system.

Nevertheless, grading *is* a relatively easy method of evaluation, and the administration generally finds it efficient. Up to now, colleges have also found grading to be a more convenient basis for selection of future students.

In terms of an equation:

History + Research + Experience = Arguments Against Traditional Grades, while
Teacher Ease + Administrative Convenience + College Admissions Procedures = Forces Which Maintain Traditional Grades.

As to the second part of your question—Is anybody doing anything about getting away from traditional grading and trying some system that will hopefully be better?—the answer is "yes." There are hundreds of colleges, secondary schools and elementary schools throughout the country which are trying alternative grading systems. I understand your faculty has a committee which is exploring alternatives to the grading system, and I imagine, at some future date, they will have a good deal of information to share with you on alternatives.

As for your last question—what I'd recommend for Mapleton High—I really can't answer that. I don't mean to beg the question. Personally, I think that traditional grading is more harmful than helpful to the learning process. But as to what Mapleton High should do, that's really up to you—the teachers, the administration, the parents, and also, although they're not here tonight, the students of Mapleton. You've got to decide for yourselves.

In closing, I'd like to read a statement from *The Handbook of Research on Teaching:*

"Considering the importance of grading for both students and instructors, it is regrettable that there is so little empirical research on it.

"How do students learn to evaluate themselves? How do they learn to set goals for themselves? Do differing grading procedures facilitate or block such learning? Can more educational substitutes for grades be devised? To these questions we have no answers at the present time." (86)

If your committee comes up with some suggestions for constructive change, I'd like you to give them thoughtful consideration. Remember, no one has ever proven that the present system is the best one, or even a good one. So maybe you people can come up with a better one. My own feeling is that you owe it to your children to try.

13 | *The Committee Examines Alternatives to Traditional Grading*

DURING THE three weeks since their first meeting, the committee had been gathering information. Cannon had arranged for Terry Hansen to become a member of the committee and, through Terry the entire grading committee from Cannon's class had been involved in the data-gathering process. Two other students were present —one selected by Mr. Collins and one by Miss Doyle— both *A* students.

Terry reminded the committee that, at their previous meeting, they had identified eight major alternatives to traditional grading. He had these alternatives on a chart, which he taped to the artificial cherrywood panelling in the administrative conference room where they were meeting.

Under Cannon's leadership and with each member contributing the information he had gathered, the committee began the serious task of reviewing and examining the eight alternatives:*

---

* A detailed summary of this meeting is included in Appendix B, which tries to present the alternatives as objectively as possible. There is probably no *one* grading system best for all situations, at all times. The rest of this chapter shows the committee discussing the alternatives for Mapleton High School only. Schools and classes considering changes in their

ALTERNATIVES TO TRADITIONAL GRADING

1. Written Evaluation
2. Self-Evaluation
3. Give grades; but don't tell the students
4. Contract System
5. The Mastery Approach or Performance Curriculum
   (Five - Point System)
6. Pass/Fail Grading (Two - Point Mastery Approach)
   a. Modified P/F
   b. Limited P/F
7. Credit/No Credit Grading
8. Blanket Grading

After the first two alternatives were described and consideration was given to their disadvantages as well as advantages, Collins said, "I'm glad to see you people are exercising a little critical thinking here. Frankly, I was afraid I was going to have to do battle with a bunch of irrational radicals."

Doris Doyle and Cliff Harper laughed and Walter Cannon and the students smiled. The "compliment" relieved the tension.

A large amount of information was presented and digested by the members. Although the pros and cons of each alternative were aired, they scrupulously avoided

grading systems will have to carefully weigh the pros and cons of each alternative with respect to *their own* situations.

Some readers will prefer to read the Appendix at this time. Others will prefer to follow along with the plot of the Mapleton High story and consider the alternatives in detail at a later time. Either approach may be taken without disservice to the story.

passing over-all value judgments on any of the alternatives. This was to be the agenda for the next meeting.

Although the meeting was long, the committee members felt good about their progress. They had set an agenda and stuck to it. They had worked together toward a common goal—culling as much information as possible on alternative grading systems. There was no factionalism, and there was even a sense of camaraderie.

At their next meeting everyone agreed that the system of giving grades but not telling them to the students would just not do for Mapleton High.

Their first dispute broke out over the alternative of written evaluations.

"I don't understand you at all, Terry," Harper said. "You're always complaining that the single letter grades don't tell you anything. And now you're saying that you don't like written evaluations either."

"I'm *not* against written evaluations," Terry answered. "I think written evaluations are a great way for a teacher to say things to a student privately and visa versa. But I'm against using written evaluations as part of a kid's permanent record, to follow him around for the rest of his life."

Terry pulled out a copy of a satire on written evaluations—the checklist variety—and passed it around the room.

TEACHER EVALUATION [1]

TEACHER *Socrates*

A. Personal Qualifications

RATING (High to Low)

	1	2	3	4	5	COMMENTS
PERSONAL APPEARANCE					✓	*Dresses in an old sheet.*
SELF-CONFIDENCE					✓	*Not sure of himself — always asking questions.*
USE OF ENGLISH				✓		*Speaks with heavy Greek accent.*
ADAPTABILITY					✓	*Prone to suicide by poison under stress.*

B. Class Management

ORGANIZATION					✓	*Does not keep a seating chart.*
ROOM APPEARANCE				✓		*Does not have eye-catching bulletin board.*
UTILIZATION OF SUPPLIES	✓					

Teacher-Pupil Relationship

TACT AND CONSIDERATION					✓	*Places students in embarrassing situation by asking questions.*
ATTITUDE OF CLASS		✓				*Class is friendly.*

• 209

D. *Techniques of Teaching*

DAILY PREPARATION — ✓ — *Does not keep daily lesson plans.*

ATTENTION TO COURSE OF STUDY — ✓ — *Quite flexible — allow students to wander to different topics.*

KNOWLEDGE OF SUBJECT MATTER — ✓ — *Does not know material has to question to gain knowledge.*

E. *Professional Attitude*

PROFESSIONAL ETHICS — ✓ — *Does not belong to professional organizatio or P.T.A.*

IN-SERVICE TRAINING — ✓ — *Complete failure here hasn't even a college degree.*

PARENT RELATIONSHIPS — ✓ — *Needs to improve — pa trying to get rid of hi*

RECOMMENDATION: *Does not have a place in Educatio Should not be rehired.*

After a bit more discussion, the committee decided that written evaluations were not the answer for Mapleton High. Harper and others felt they just didn't have the time to write out meaningful evaluations for 130 students, more or less, four times a year.

The discussions on self-evaluation and self-grading, the contract system, and blanket grading were heated, but all ended with the same conclusion: these might be excellent alternatives for teachers to try out in their own classrooms, but they just would not work, in the long run, in all classes, during four years of high school. One or two of the committee members disagreed, but none of these alternatives seemed to hold the whole committee's interest as the possible solution they were looking for.

The five-point mastery approach to grading *did* capture their interest. Collins felt this alternative would help make grading more meaningful and objective. If teachers would only state their objectives, devise ways of measuring them, designate various performance levels and so on, grading would be a more defensible practice.

Again, Terry disagreed. "OK. I'll grant that you can make grading more scientific. You can get students working toward clearly defined goals and you can find ways to measure our performance. We won't be able to complain that our grades aren't fair. But don't you see? *You* are still setting our goals for us. When do we learn to set *our own* goals? What do you think we kids are rebelling against anyway? With your scientific grading, I'd feel even more like a rat in a maze than I do now."

That comment set off an argument that lasted for ten minutes, then Walter Cannon brought up a new point.

"You know, I like this performance curriculum idea. But, frankly, I don't know how to set up this mastery approach. I know enough about it to know it's a complicated business. It's still an area for curriculum specialists for the most part. Oh, I guess we can get some help and learn how to do this scientifically, but I just don't think there are the funds or the commitment around here to undertake such a big project. This mastery approach implies changing not only grading but our whole style of teaching. It's just too big a step for us to undertake right now."

The other members agreed. They had discussed six of the alternatives, and they did not feel comfortable recommending any of them to the entire Mapleton High School faculty.

"Wait a minute," Cannon said. "We already agreed that my blanket grading system might work in one classroom but could not be applied to the whole school. But if it *can* work in one classroom, then maybe it can work throughout the entire school in the form of pass/fail grading. Instead of *B* or *F*, you'd have *P* or *F*."

"Could you explain the meaning of pass/fail grading?" Gail asked.

"Sure," Mr. Cannon said. "At the beginning of the course, the teacher states his criteria for passing. Any student who meets these criteria passes; any student who does not, fails. A student does not have to whine or argue for the two points that will bring up his grade one letter; he does not have to cheat to get a *B* instead of a *C* or an *A* instead of a *B*. Beyond the level of passing, he can explore the course in his own way, exercising as much creativity as he wishes . . ."

"Couldn't a teacher still fail a student for being too creative?" Joel Brown interrupted.

"It's possible," Terry admitted, "but not likely. Take me, for example. I usually do *A* or *B* work. If I tried something different in a class now and a teacher didn't like it, he might give me a low *B* or a *C*. So I'm scared to try some creative things, because I don't want to take the chance unless I'm positive I can pull it off. But with *P* or *F,* I don't think any teacher would fail me if I made an effort to meet the agreed upon criteria. Then I'd feel free to experiment, to set some of my own educational goals and ways of meeting them."

Mr. Cannon added, "One of the corollaries of pass/fail grading is that if the student receives a failing mark he gets a chance to do his work over to bring it up to passing quality. In this sense, pass/fail grading is a form of mastery approach, with two levels instead of five. Any student who masters the course receives a passing grade.

"Another advantage is that pass/fail grading eliminates most of the need for unhealthy competition, pressure on students, cheating and apple-polishing. The only students who would still have a need for these techniques would be those in danger of failing. So, for most students the focus of education could then return to learning, where it should be."

"I guess this makes a certain amount of sense," Russ Collins conceded, "but isn't it unfair to our better students? Those students who excel in a given subject should be recognized. By not having a special category to denote exceptional performance, aren't you taking away an added stimulus to motivate them?"

"Many of the colleges experimenting with pass/fail grading have a 'modified pass/fail' plan whereby they have some special category to designate the outstanding students," Cannon informed them. "The most common modified system is the *H/P/F* system (Honors/Pass /Fail). Personally, I think the straight pass/fail is better.

"You raised two points, Russ. One was that the outstanding student deserved to be recognized. By that, I assume you mean mainly for college admissions. The other was that the chance for an outstanding grade would motivate him to do outstanding work.

"I agree with you that we want to be able to identify our outstanding students to help them get into college; but this is the purpose of letters of recommendation. Any teacher who could give a student an *H* should be able to write a reference that would be helpful to his getting into the college of his choice.

"As to your second point about motivation, I don't think grades motivate learning at all. 'Grading *does* motivate cramming, and conning, and fretting, and cheating and the appearance of education. They may produce some activity—which should not be confused with education. Grades assure a vicious distortion of motivation.'[2] Any student who works for an *H* is not an outstanding student at all. He is an authority authority-pleaser, a grade grubber and a person who very much needs to

214 •

begin developing his *own* values."

"I don't like the *H* for another reason," Gail added. "If I really worked in most courses, I could probably get an *H*. But in a lot of courses, I wouldn't *want* to work for an *H*. I'd want to devote my energies to courses which really interest me. Someone should work hard in a subject because he likes it, not just to get an *H*. But if the *H* was a possibility, I'd feel compelled to work for it even though I knew I'd learn more important things doing something else."

"That makes a lot of sense," Doris Doyle agreed. "Motivation should come from within. That was the point of MacIntyre's speech, remember? We'll recognize our outstanding students and will certainly let the colleges know of their outstanding work."

"Where is this pass/fail system being practiced?" Harper asked. "We hear a lot about it, but who's doing it, and how is it working out?"

Terry leafed through his papers, found what he was looking for and said, "The students on my committee gathered a lot of information about this, so I think I can answer your question, Mr. Harper. There must be hundreds of places that have introduced pass/fail grading. For example, the Phi Beta Kappa people surveyed 121 of their chapters and learned that 97 of those institutions had some sort of pass/fail system.[3]

"More and more colleges are converting to pass/fail all the time. At Caltech, the Dean reported that 'the sophomore performance of the first pass/fail class of freshmen was better than that of previous sophomore classes . . . there was a significantly-improved attitude toward learning, for reasons other than grades.' [4]

"Some junior high schools and high schools have begun to introduce pass/fail and credit/no credit grading. The high schools have come last because they've been fearful that their students would have trouble getting into colleges if they didn't have grades."

"Well, we've finally gotten to the major point," Russ Collins stated. "As I understand it, colleges want *grades* from their applicants. They have a large number of applications and they want every available piece of information."

"Well," Terry said, "what they want and what they'll accept may be two different things. Sure they'd prefer grades, but from what we found out, *most colleges will accept applicants without grades, and they will not be prejudiced against these applicants.*"

"That's a pretty important piece of information," Collins said. "Do you have the research facts?"

"Well, sir, among our sources are several public and private high schools that have eliminated grades and have surveyed the colleges to be sure this change would not harm their graduates who seek college entrance. For example, the John Dewey High School, a large, experimental public school in New York City, surveyed all the colleges in the New York area and found that the 'lack of grades would not be detrimental' to their students' entrance. In addition, they report the following: 'We 'are forwarding information about John Dewey High School to colleges throughout the country. So far, our response has been quite positive. Consequently, though we do not guarantee admission to college for every one of our students, we are hopeful that our students will not have difficulty in entering schools of higher learning throughout the country.'[5]

"The several large, public high schools which conducted their own surveys would not have done away with grades without some pretty solid evidence to ensure that their students would not be hurt by such a change.

"We ourselves have also conducted an informal survey by talking with admissions officers and writing letters to colleges. The essential question we asked them was: 'If you received an application from a high school student who attended a school that did not give grades, but you did receive that student's SAT scores (plus other standardized test scores he might have received), letters of recommendation, a few samples of the student's work, and had an interview with the student, would his application receive the same consideration as those applications from students applying from schools that do give grades and class rank?'

"On the basis of the formal and informal answers we have received to that question from colleges across the nation, we have obtained the following information: About one third of the colleges said they foresaw absolutely no problem with such an application. The majority of colleges replied that although the application would create some problems for the admissions office, they did not think this would be harmful to the student. Only a very small percentage replied that, given their present policies regarding admissions qualifications, an application submitted without grades would be or might be detrimental to the student. This, then, is our second reason for claiming that the elimination of grades does not pose an insoluble problem in terms of college admissions.[6, 7]

"Finally, our third reason for this claim is the historical trend we see developing. Let's go back a few years. When colleges were considering the elimination of traditional grading, they were worried that graduate schools would not accept their students. But they eliminated grades anyway, and no major problems arose. Now, more and more colleges are moving away from traditional grading. High schools are starting to do the same, but, as yet, on a limited basis. As more and more colleges welcome students from schools without grades, then more and more high schools will eliminate traditional grading.

"The question is whether we at Mapleton High want to be among the first high schools to make the move or whether we want to lag behind and continue, dissatisfied, with a system that is difficult to justify."

"You ought to be a lawyer, son," Collins said. The room remained quiet for a while.

"Perhaps I should summarize now for clarification," Cannon offered. "We discussed pass/fail grading, and heard the arguments in favor of this system. Most people felt that pass/fail grading was better than the modified pass/fail (*H/P/F*). Terry presented his committee's reasons why they do not believe the elimination of traditional grades would jeopardize Mapleton graduates' chances for college admissions.

"So far, pass/fail grading is the alternative that has seemed to capture our interest the most. Maybe we should talk about whether or not we want pass/fail for Mapleton High."

"Before we do that, Walter," Miss Doyle interrupted, "can we talk a bit about credit/no credit grading?"

"I agree," Terry said. "Pass/fail and credit/no credit are similar in many ways, so maybe it makes more sense to see which is *better* for Mapleton High. Is that right, Miss Doyle?"

Miss Doyle smiled at Terry. "That's just what I was thinking. Am I correct in thinking that the only difference between pass/fail and credit/no credit is that, under the latter system, the student does not fail. If he passes the course, *CR* (credit) is noted on his transcript. If he does not pass the course, an *NC* (no credit) is noted, which simply means he did not get credit. It might mean he dropped the course, got sick, didn't pass or whatever—but there is no connotation of failure. Is that right?"

"That's right," Cannon said.

"This system seems to make more sense than pass/fail. If you carry pass/fail to its logical end, you come to credit/no credit. Why penalize the student for failing?" Doris questioned.

"The better students don't have to worry about failing, but a lot of the girls I talk to in my home ec classes *do*. Why penalize *them?* If working under too much pressure is supposed to be detrimental to learning, why put these kids under the fear of failing? If cheating and apple-polishing will save them from an *F,* why give them that temptation?

"I think we should talk about credit/no credit instead of pass/fail. It seems to have all of the advantages of pass/fail without some of the disadvantages. Terry, is credit/no credit being used much these days?"

"Oh, yes. It's not as popular as pass/fail, but dozens of schools are using it."

"Well, I like it," Miss Doyle said. "What do you all think? I think that credit/no credit grading is the best alternative for Mapleton High."

The room became tense almost immediately. People avoided each other's glances. For the first time, the committee had to deal with the major question: did they plan to make any recommendations for a new grading system for Mapleton High? Criticizing the various alternatives was one thing; going before the faculty with a proposal for change was another.

"I like it, too," Gail Redcay said. "If we want to get credit for our courses, we'll have to do the work. But we won't have to work for a grade. We could work to please ourselves. And cheating and telling the teacher what he wants to hear wouldn't be rewarded. It would be so much more relaxed and fun to come to school."

"Well, I wouldn't go *that* far," Terry said. "I don't know if credit/no credit could make school fun, but it could surely relieve some of the problems. Personally, I think it's the best alternative."

"I see one problem," Cliff Harper interjected. "If grades are eliminated, then the College Board scores will be much more important. How are you students going to feel knowing that your admission to college is going to be based, to a large extent, on the score of that one test?"

"That's a problem I hadn't considered," Cannon observed.

"Good point, Harper," Collins said.

"I'd rather have to deal with that one SAT score, than be hit over the head with grades all my school life and have them ruin my education," Terry said. "Anyway, I don't think it's quite as serious as you make it sound. You can take the SAT's over again if you really bomb them the first time. And if.the teachers care to they can write to the colleges explaining that your work over the years has been a lot better than your SAT's indicate. Also, part of our idea is for each student to have a portfolio of work he's done in high school. If a student has impressive material in his portfolio, this could compensate for low scores on SAT's. He could also include other scores on nationally-recognized tests. At any rate, I just can't see sacrificing four years of high school to the grading system just because I might panic and get a low score on the SAT's."

"I think that's a good point, Terry," Harper said. "I still think credit/no credit will put heavier emphasis on SAT scores, and this is a disadvantage; but I agree that the advantages of eliminating traditional grading far outweigh the disadvantages. I'm decidedly in favor of credit/no credit."

"Well," Cannon said. "That's four for credit/no credit. What about you, Russ? And *you,* Joel? You haven't said much."

"I've been thinking everything over," Joel said. "To tell the truth, I don't think credit/no credit will change anything very much. Some kids will still try to please the teacher, and some will still not do any work . . ."

"I agree with Joel," Collins said. "I admit there are some good arguments in favor of pass/fail and credit/no credit, but I'm not so sure they're going to be that much better than the present system. I also see some problems. For example, if a student can drop a course at any time, without fear of failure, you might have kids dropping courses at whim, without telling anyone, and then taking forever to graduate from high school; we wouldn't know where kids were at any given time during the day; we . . ."

"Wait a minute, Russ. Wait a minute." Cannon's impatience was obvious. "The colleges with credit/no credit have apparently managed to solve these difficulties, so I'm sure *we* could develop guidelines to make the plan workable. If we can juggle around 2,000 students, 150 teachers, a hundred or so rooms, flexible scheduling, four grade levels, three ability groups, and so on, to keep Mapleton High running smoothly, then surely we can make a few rules and guidelines to take care of the problems you raise."

"I guess that's right, Walter, but for some reason, I just can't buy the idea. And I'm sure I'm not the only teacher. This committee's one thing, but if you try to get the whole school onto a credit/no credit system, you're going to fail. It's too big a step. The faculty won't go for it; neither will the parents."

Harper's eyes happened to meet Cannon's as Russ Collins spoke. As they looked at each other, each knew, and each knew the other knew, that Collins was speaking the truth. Miss Doyle and Mr. Harper had not entered the committee with their minds made up; but they were open to new ideas. They were not fearful of change. Many faculty members were more cautious. They had not been through the process of investigating and weighing all the alternatives. And despite Dr. Miller's visit and the recent PTA meeting, many were still solidly in favor of traditional grading. Recommending a complete shift to credit/no credit—one that would force all teachers and students to give up traditional grading—would surely meet with defeat.

"You know," Harper said, "most of the colleges experimenting with pass/fail and credit/no credit have done so on a limited basis. At Penn State, for example, students were allowed to take up to 18 hours on a pass/fail basis. At Harvard, students could take one out of four courses as pass/fail. At some schools students could take pass/fail courses only outside their major. Since many high schools are doing this too, couldn't we also set up credit/no credit grading on a limited basis?"

"I'm sure we could, Cliff," Walter Cannon agreed, "and the proposal would have a better chance of being accepted by the faculty, which is better than nothing. But from what we found out about limited pass/fail and credit/no credit grading, they just don't go far enough it seems to me.

"For example, if a student can take *some* of his courses on a pass/fail basis, the importance of his traditionally graded courses in determining his overall average increases. As with the SAT's we were discussing before, taking the pressure off students in some courses *increases* the pressure in his other courses."

"And remember, Mr. Cannon," Terry added, "another problem we found was that students would manipulate their pass/fail options to get better grades. For example, students wouldn't take easy courses on a pass/fail basis, even though they felt they could enjoy them more if they did. Students would save their pass/fail options for harder courses. Also, although this is not the intent of the system, the pass/fail courses would be regarded by the students as less important than the graded courses."

"I see what you mean," Harper said. "Only when the student's *whole program* is graded credit/no credit can he really be free of the grading game."

"Right. I feel very strongly that limited pass/fail hurts as much as it helps, because it gives the illusion of change while maintaining the same essential grading system."

"That may be true," Russ Collins said, "but you're still going to have a hell of a time selling an all-or-nothing plan to the Mapleton faculty. You'll end up with nothing."

Cannon turned to Collins and spoke slowly, carefully framing his thoughts as he talked. "Russ, if we were to come up with a plan that would allow teachers and students the opportunity to choose which plan—credit/no credit or traditional grading—they wished to operate under, could you support such a proposal?"

"You mean some teachers would give traditional grades and some credit/no credit?"

"Yes, according to their own choice."

"And students would also choose?"

"Yes, with their parents' permission, of course."

"Hmm. Well, yes, I think I might be able to go along with that. Only it sounds a bit chaotic. It would have to be worked out pretty carefully. That kind of thing could really backfire if badly planned."

"But if it *were* well-planned, and if teachers and students were allowed the freedom to choose, would you support it as an experimental alternative?"

"Well, of course, I'd have to know all the details first, but I think I could support such a plan. As long as the students don't get hurt by it, and you're not forcing anyone to operate under credit/no credit. But why are you asking? Do you have anything specific in mind?"

"Yes, I think I do. I'd like to work out the details first with the aid of Terry's committee. I'd like to suggest we meet again next week—same time, same place. OK with all of you? Great. I think I may have the alternative that the faculty will accept and which will allow those students who want credit/no credit to have their whole program graded that way."

"Well, you've sure created enough suspense," Doris Doyle said. "I certainly hope the plan is worth the waiting."

"I think it will be, Doris. Anyone need a ride home?"

14 | *A Recommendation for Change*

THE ENTIRE FACULTY, over four hundred students and about one hundred parents—most of them mothers—filed into the auditorium for the 3:30 meeting that mid-March afternoon. Predictably, the hundreds of little conversations going on throughout the room were all on the same topic.

"Well, something is finally going to *happen* around this school."

"I've heard they're going to do away with grades."

"Watch carefully, Al. You are about to see the student body sold out."

"I bet you a dollar nothing is going to change."

"I hope they know what they're doing. I'm not going to go along with any plan that's going to jeopardize my daughter's chances for college."

"Have you heard anything *specific*? All I've heard have been rumors. The committee sure has been secretive. You'd think it was the Paris Peace talks going on."

"Well, I hope their deliberations will be more *productive*!"

Actually, only thirteen people—Mr. Cunningham, his vice-principal, two guidance counselors, the Superintendent of Schools, the head of the Board of Education, and of course, the seven members of the Committee—knew what was in the Committee's report.

At the third meeting of the Committee, as planned, Walter Cannon had presented his idea to the others, and it met with their hearty approval. Even Russ Collins was pleased. "As far as I can see," he said, "you're not forcing any teachers or students into this experiment, and the whole thing seems quite workable, although it's going to make scheduling a bit more complicated."

After that, the Committee brought its proposal to Mr. Cunningham, who suggested some changes and invited his assistant principal and two members of the guidance staff to look it over and react. Their response was similar to that of Mr. Collins. It was a good compromise. It would allow those teachers and students against traditional grades to be free from them, while allowing any students and parents who wanted traditional grades to continue to receive them. It *would* be possible to schedule, although the guidance staff would have to work over-time, in the summer, to hammer out all the details.

The next step was to bring the proposal to the Superintendent of Schools and the Chairman of the Board of Education. They agreed with the educational wisdom of the idea, but they were concerned with the community's reaction. Would they go along with it? Would it stir up the kind of controversy they would all regret later? Would they be willing to allow an experiment that might—even if the odds were against it—create a problem when their children applied to college?

"But that's the beauty of the plan," argued Walter Cannon who was with Mr. Cunningham at the meeting. "Any parent who objects to this plan does not have to give his child permission to transfer to the credit/no credit track. This proposal will not interfere with their children's education or chances for college in any way whatsoever. There's nothing they can really object to. If they want their children to be part of the experiment, that's their free choice. If they are scared or if they're against the plan, then it's their choice not to participate in it."

Finally, the superintendent and the Chairman of the Board of Education said they did not see anything basically wrong with the proposal and that they would support it, as long as Mr. Cunningham used discretion in its implementation and made every effort to keep the community fully informed.

As Joseph Cunningham banged the gavel to call the meeting to order, the events of the past months flashed swiftly through his mind. He thought of all the meetings, the enthusiasm that had been generated in a large number of the faculty and the students, the intense interest the parents had shown in Dr. Standish's PTA presentation, and the tinge of excitement—mixed with some anxiety—he had felt being the man in charge of the school that was considering becoming one of the pioneers in American education. To his own surprise, he felt himself hoping that the Committee's proposal would be overwhelmingly accepted by the faculty. In the beginning he had not been very interested in changing the grading system, but during the last few weeks he had come to regard the Committee's report as also his own.

"Members of the faculty, parents and students," he began, when the auditorium quieted down, "I am pleased to see so many of you here today, which indicates to me your concern about the quality of education we are trying to provide here at Mapleton High. I think each of us has basically the same goal in mind— to make this the best possible high school we can.

"As perhaps you've noticed," he cleared his throat, "the issue of grading has been the topic of discussion, and even controversy, for us this year. Over the last few months, many students, faculty members and parents have become concerned that the traditional grading system, (using *A, B, C* and so on) may not be the most effective way to evaluate students. Many people feel that traditional grades can, in some cases, even be harmful to the educational process. No one has proved that the traditional grading system is the best way of evaluating and reporting student progress, nor has anyone proved that another system would definitely be better. It's a baffling problem.

"A student-faculty committee was appointed to investigate alternatives to our present grading system. The committee was asked to inform us of the alternatives available, what the advantages and disadvantages of each alternative are, and what recommendations, if any, they would make for Mapleton High School. I know many of us have been waiting eagerly for this report, so I would like to turn the meeting over to Walter Cannon of our Social Studies Department who will present the Committee's report."

At least a hundred students, led by "Cannon's 17," gave Cannon a resounding round of applause. But he did not seemed pleased.

"We're here for a serious purpose today. We're here to consider changing a practice that has been central to the life of our school. I hope we can all be thoughtful and even introspective, rather than acting as though we're at a football game . . .

"I would like to begin by saying that I am speaking this afternoon for the entire Committee on Alternatives to the Grading System, which includes Mr. Clifford Harper, Mr. Russell Collins, Miss Doris Doyle, Mr. Terry Hansen, Miss Gail Redcay, Mr. Joel Brown and myself.

"And I am very pleased to say that the report and recommendations I am presenting are offered as the *unanimous* decision of the Committee. Of course, we differed on several points along the way, and there is still some disagreement about grading; but, as far as our final report and recommendations are concerned, we are in agreement.

Mr. Cannon then proceeded to review the pros and cons of the grading alternatives discussed at the Committee's second meeting. After reviewing the eight alternatives, he said, "And so we saw two possible directions to go to improve our grading system. One direction was toward the more specific and more complicated perform-ance curriculum or mastery approach toward grading. The other was toward credit/no credit grading, which is a modified version of the mastery approach. With the standard mastery approach, five levels of performance (*A, B, C, D and F*) are specified. With credit/no credit, only two levels are specified. We agreed that Mapleton does not have the resources to implement the 5-level mastery approach properly, but that with a good deal of work, we could successfully implement the 2-level ap-proach. Our proposal, which I will present shortly, sug-gests what we will have to do to implement successfully the 2-level mastery approach.

"We concluded, then, that if we wanted to make any meaningful improvements in the grading process and related educational practices, it would have to be in the direction of credit/no credit grading. For the reasons already stated, we feel that credit/no credit grading would not seriously jeopardize any student's chances for college admissions. Most of us also feel that credit/no credit grading could significantly improve the quality of education at Mapleton High.

"However, we were not in unanimous agreement on this last point. Even if we were, we recognized that there would probably be many faculty members, students and parents who would not favor a change from traditional grading to credit/no credit grading. Our proposal, which we hope will please both those who would like to move away from traditional grading and those who would like to maintain it, was designed to meet three criteria:

1. To allow freedom of choice to teachers, students and parents. Teachers and students should be able to work under a grading system that they feel is most in harmony with their goals and teaching or learning styles.

2. To not jeopardize any student's chances for college admission.

3. To be practical and feasible, in terms of the staffing and scheduling realities of Mapleton High School.

"I would now like to present to you our recommendation for Mapleton High School:

THE COMMITTEE'S RECOMMENDATION

1. In September of the coming school year, Mapleton High will convert to a 'Two Track Grading System.' One track will be traditional grading (A, B, C, D, F); the other track, grading on a credit/no credit (CR/NC) basis.

2. As soon as possible this spring, teachers and students will indicate whether they would like to be part of the traditional grading or the CR/NC track. Students must have parental permission—

signed and kept on record in the guidance office—
to participate in the *CR/NC* grading.

3. A student must choose one track or the other. He
cannot take some of his courses on a *CR/NC*
basis and others on a traditional grading basis. If
this were allowed, students might manipulate their
credit/no credit options in an attempt to raise
their average (taking only hard courses on a
credit/no credit basis, for example); and this
would defeat the purpose of the new system.

4. A teacher may elect to teach some of his courses
in the traditional grading manner and others
using the credit/no credit system. Thus, a teacher
himself can experiment to see which he prefers.

5. By using this method, classes can be organized
in which the teacher and all the students have
chosen the same grading system. Presumably, this
agreement upon the grading system will help to
establish an initial rapport between teacher and
students, as well as to eliminate many of the arguments over grading philosophies which often take
place in classrooms.

6. A perfect matching of student and teacher choices
will be impossible. In some cases there might be
more students wanting to be in the *CR/NC* track
than there are teachers to teach *CR/NC* courses.
For example, if one third of the students elect
CR/NC grading, this would be enough to fill
about 27 English classes. But if the number of
English teachers who desire to use *CR/NC* can
only cover 23 classes, 4 classes, or 100 students, are

without a teacher to teach them English under the *CR/NC* system. In this case, these 100 students will have to be in English classes using the traditional grading system.

However, all is not lost. A common practice at many colleges which use a limited credit/no credit or pass/fail system is to have their teachers assign grades as usual but not record those grades for students who are taking the course as a pass/fail option. In other words, those 100 students would receive grades from their teachers, but the guidance office would change the *A*'s, *B*'s and *C*'s into *CR*'s on the students' transcripts, and the *D*'s and *F*'s into *NC*'s.

This is not an ideal situation. It would be better if *all* the classes could be composed of teachers and students who have chosen the same grading system. But this is impossible, if people are to be given a choice. At least under this plan, *all* students who elect to can have *CR/NC* grading.

7. Conceivably, student and teacher choice could create the opposite situation to the one just discussed. Perhaps *more* teachers than students might want to use the *CR/NC* grading. The smaller the department or the fewer the number of sections of a course, the more likely this would be. For example, we offer six physics classes this year. One teacher teaches four of them; another teacher teaches the other two. The teacher with four classes might want to use *CR/NC* grading; but if only 50 physics students want *CR/NC* grading the teacher will have to be willing to compromise. He

can have two classes to teach with the *CR/NC* system, but the other two will have to be graded traditionally.

Cannon stopped and looked up from his papers. "Do you get the picture so far? I've presented the *overall* design for the 'Two-Track Grading System.' But how would this look in the individual classrooms?" He looked down and began reading again.

8. In order to make evaluations and the reporting of progress more meaningful, in *all* courses—credit/ no credit and traditioning grading—the following plan will be implemented: [2]

   a. Copies of specific course objectives will be dis tributed to and discussed with students at the beginning of each course.

   b. These objectives will be the basis for evaluations, progress reports and grades in each course.

   c. Students will write their own self-evaluations based on the specified course objectives, as well as their own personal goals, as they relate to the course. Teachers will read these and return them to the students with appropriate written comments.

   d. Student-teacher conferences are encouraged when needed.

   e. Reports to counselors and parents will include these student-teacher evaluations.

f. These reports will be sent to counselors and parents every marking period. Additional reports may be sent as needed. This would eliminate the need for the present 'warning letter.'

g. These student-teacher evaluations will be kept on file in the guidance office to assist students, parents and counselors in the process of college and vocational guidance. They will *not,* under any circumstances, be sent to colleges or employers.

9. In traditionally-graded courses, in addition to the student-teacher evaluations, a letter grade will be submitted for each student each marking period. For students in the traditionally-graded track, these grades will become part of their permanent transcripts, to be computed into a cumulative average and sent to colleges, as usual.

10. When a student from the credit/no credit track applies to colleges or seeks employment, the following information will be sent to admissions or personnel offices:

a. An explanation of the school's credit/no credit system.

b. A transcript showing those courses for which the student received credit *and* a list of the course objectives for each course mentioned.

c. Letters of recommendation from five teachers chosen by the student. Teachers will be encouraged to include in their letters specific descriptive statements regarding the student's work.

d. Scholastic Aptitude Test (SAT) scores, as well as any other standardized test scores the student and counselor feel should be included.

e. Whenever possible, the student will visit the college or employer for a personal interview.

f. The student's portfolio (described below).

11. The student in the CR/NC track will keep a portfolio of products he and his teachers feel are representative of his work. English and history papers, photographs of science projects, tape recordings of recitals, a letter from the advisor of the math club describing the student's record in 'math meets,' art work, and so on could be placed in the portfolio. When the time comes to apply to college, the student and his parents, working with the advisor and the teachers, will select the work they feel would be representative and, hopefully, impressive. Copies will be sent to the colleges. Obviously, not all admissions offices will read the papers or go over all the materials; but the portfolio will, nevertheless, put the student in a good light. A written description of the contents of the portfolio will accompany the student's application. If the admissions officer does not go through the portfolio completely, at least he will be aware of its contents.

At this point, Cannon looked out across the auditorium. "I've been taking one point after another here.

Everyone is so quiet. I can't tell whether you're totally interested or now you're falling asleep. Do any of you have questions . . . Yes, Mrs. Wagner?"

"The proposal sounds very interesting, Mr. Cannon, but is it really practical? I believe that was your second criterion—to be practical. Can it be scheduled?"

Cannon looked over to where Ben Crowell, the head of the Guidance Department, was sitting. "Mr. Crowell, you'd probably be better able to answer that than I."

"Well, I wouldn't exactly say that we're looking forward to scheduling this kind of thing, but if that's what the faculty wants, we can do it—it's just going to take extra time. Essentially, it's no different from the kind of scheduling we do now, when we have about 15 thousand student-choices for courses, about 600 courses to schedule for teachers, and about 100 rooms to put you all in. This new variable won't create a new headache; it'll just make our present one somewhat more painful."

"Thanks, Ben," Cannon said. "I wish I could offer you an easy aspirin for it. Yes, Mr. Ingles?"

"I don't know whether you've foreseen all the problems this kind of plan might get us into. For example, if a student doesn't have to worry about an *F* on his record, what's to prevent his taking eight years to finish high school? In fact, he might stay in high school until he's 26, just to avoid the draft. Do you want to encourage this kind of thing?"

"As a matter of fact, we have thought about these

possibilities. Our committee discussed a lot of them. For example, without traditional grades, when does a student become ineligible to participate in a varsity sport? At present, if he has below a *C* average, he cannot participate. And what about the Honor Society? Students now need a 90 average or better. To keep good students who are working under the credit/no credit plan out of the Honor Society would not be fair. And what about students who transfer to and from other school districts? And what about the valedictorian, traditionally the student with the highest average?

"It would be necessary to devise a new set of rules and guidelines. This would not be difficult. We might say, for example, that no student may take more than five years to complete high school. If he does, he has to do so in night school. Perhaps a student-faculty board might be appointed or elected to select the valedictorian. Any student who submits a valedictory address to the committee would be eligible. The committee would select the most interesting speech to be read, which, in fact, might be a much better method of selecting valedictorians.

"Although this new grading system would require new regulations, in some cases we might even find more creative ways to make decisions than we've used in the past."

"Mr. Cannon?"

"Yes, Barry."

"Under this new system, could we switch in mid-year

or between years, from one plan to the other?"

"There would have to be a rule that no student could switch from one grading system to another in the middle of the year. A student's schedule is built around the grading track he's in. If he changed grading tracks, he'd have to have his schedule completely revised.

"However, it *would* be possible for a student (and of course, a teacher) to change grading tracks at the end of the year. In the spring, when course choices are made, he could choose to be in a different track in September. My hope is that students wouldn't jump back and forth very much. Hopefully, they would find the right track for themselves and stay in it. But, we see no reason to prevent changing.

"If a student spent three years in the traditional grading track and his senior year in the *CR/NC* track, we would send his three-year average to the colleges and notify them that he received credit for his senior courses. If he did some outstanding work, we might send a copy of that along, too—a mini-portfolio, you might say. Similarly, if he spent his first two years in the traditional grading track, we'd send his two-year average, plus the portfolio and *CR* notations for the last two years.

"We do see the need for a guideline here, though. We were worried that a student who had an unusually good year in the ninth grade might switch to credit/no credit just so his average could be that of this *one year*. We decided that if a student converted to *CR/NC* grading in his sophomore year and stayed with it throughout high school, then his freshman year grades would be translated into *CR/NC* notations.

"Now, when you asked whether we could switch from this system in mid-year or at the end of a year, your 'we' might have referred to our *whole school*. And, for the same reasons an individual could not switch in midstream, the entire school couldn't either. We would have to completely revise the entire school's schedule, and we'd probably have no more than a weekend to do it in. I could see that turning Ben Crowell's headache into a stroke." The auditorium broke into laughter. Cannon relaxed a bit and went on.

"But we certainly could change at the end of a year, if there were serious problems in the system. I think, however, this would be a mistake. Often the impact of a change, the results of an experiment, take some time to be seen. Students have worked under the system of letter grading for so long, and teachers have used this system for so long, it may take a while for the change to feel comfortable and workable. It may take a whole year of learning from our mistakes before we begin to make progress. I'd be sorry to see our experiment end prematurely.

"As long as we've raised this question of the *experiment*, let me say a little about that. Our committee feels we could learn a great deal about the teaching and learning process from this kind of experiment. We think it would be a good idea to call in some research people and ask them to help us design a plan which would enable us to measure our results. For our own sake and so that others might profit from our findings, research *is* something we should consider. Mr. Cunningham has indicated that potential funds are available.

"Thinking back to those three criteria I mentioned at the beginning, you, I hope, will agree that this plan meets those criteria. Both the teachers and the students are given a free choice. Our plan will not jeopardize the student's college admission, and we think it's workable.

"I want to emphasize that a new grading system will not solve all our educational problems. Questions about the curriculum, instructional methods, under-achievement, student participation in decision making, faculty-student relations—all these issues and others will continue to plague us. But a new method of evaluation *can* help free us from the grading game which presently consumes so much of our time and energy that we never get around to *dealing* with those other educational problems. Mr. Cunningham, will you take over now?"

There was loud and enthusiastic applause for Cannon as he strode down the steps from the stage.

"So now we come to the $64 question," Cunningham began. "You've heard the committee's report and recommendation. The question is: do you, as a faculty, wish to accept this recommendation and institute the suggested 'Two Track Grading System' at Mapleton High?"

Since the faculty wanted time to think it over and discuss it further, Mr. Ingles made a motion to postpone the decision for a week, and the motion was passed.

By the next Monday, the teachers were all talked out. They had discussed little else, other than the recommendation, in and out of class, all week. The students were solidly behind the proposal. They had a choice and they were content. Many parents had mixed feelings, and discussions in many homes across Mapleton that week frequently turned into arguments.

"Over my dead body you'll take credit/no credit."

"Well, it's nice to see that change can come about without occupying buildings and sitting in offices."

"Mark my words, the experiment won't last a year."

"This is about the best thing the school's done since we moved out here."

"But, ma . . ."

Pressure from the students was clearly influencing the teachers. Many of the teachers were in favor of the plan from the beginning—once they saw that it was workable and safe, in terms of colleges. Some were against it from the beginning, however, and were hard to move. Either they were unconvinced that the present grading system was a problem, or they didn't believe this new plan would be any better. Many teachers were undecided. With these teachers the students in favor of the plan had the greatest impact.

"Look, if *you* can give grades in your classes, then why are you against my being in another class and *not* getting grades?"

"Because I'm concerned that your education will

suffer. You won't do any work."

"Oh, yes I will. At the beginning of the year the teacher has to tell us his requirements for us to get credit for the course. If I don't do the required work, I'm not going to get credit."

"But your work might be of poor quality."

"Our bio class talked with Mr. Harper about that. He said if anyone turned work into him which he felt was poor, he'd hand it back and make the kid do it over again. In that way, no one gets credit for the course unless they really earn it."

"Well, I don't know."

When the faculty meeting rolled around, no one had much to say. A few teachers spoke out in favor of the plan, and one or two against it; but the meeting lacked the excitement one would expect to see among a faculty on the verge of making such an important decision. One teacher asked Cunningham what kinds of reactions he'd been getting from the community.

"About half and half, I'd say. One half likes the idea or calls to say that even though they wouldn't want their child to be in the credit/no credit track this year, they still think the idea is a good one. The other half sounds suspicious or angry when they call—usually because they don't understand the proposal. Then, after I explain to them why they don't have anything to worry about, they seem satisfied. So I'd say the community's reaction has been pretty good. At least, *I'm* not worrying about it."

Finally, Russ Collins said, "Look, nobody is saying anything new. We've talked enough about this. Let's vote. I'd just like to say what my position is. I was on the Committee on Alternatives, as you know, and I did a lot of thinking about this issue. You couldn't have been much more pro-grades than I, in September. Except maybe for *you*, Henry." The faculty laughed, and Henry Crewson snorted at his friend Collins.

"Well, I'm still pro-grades. At least I'd prefer to teach courses with regular grading next year—well, in at least four of my five classes, anyway. But I'm not so sure about the issue any more. I think Cannon and Harper and you others, and a lot of the kids have some good points, too. I'd like to give them a chance, just to see. There are plenty of kids (or their parents) who still want grades, so I'm not worried about being put out of a job. I'm going to vote in favor of the recommendation. I hope you do, too."

The vote was 3 to 1 in favor of the Committee's recommendation. It was somewhat anti-climatic. The faculty, more than the students or parents, knew this was not the end but, rather, a beginning. They knew what it would take to organize the "Two Track Grading System." They sensed all the problems that would have to be worked out—the unforseen ones as well as those already identified. They knew how much work Cunningham would have to do to be sure every parent and student was fully informed of the change. September seemed a long way off, but if they were to plan adequately, work to implement the recommendation would have to begin at once.

After the faculty meeting, some of the students in Cannon's fourth period history class were standing by his door, waiting for him when he returned to his room to get his coat. He simply nodded his head to them, and they understood. They all walked him to his car. It was a strangely silent procession through the empty halls and out to the parking lot. Terry Hansen was closest to Cannon as he got into his car. Cannon rolled down the window. "Thanks," Terry said.

"See you tomorrow," Cannon answered, grinding the gears slightly as he shifted into first, and then drove off.

Appendices

Appendix A

SELECTED ANNOTATED BIBLIOGRAPHY RELATED TO GRADES

This list of references is not designed to be exhaustive. Rather, it is to provide the interested reader with the opportunity to review in greater detail information generated from questions surrounding the grading issue. The bibliography is divided into areas of general concern to parents, students and teachers.

I. THE ACCURACY OF GRADES—THE SUBJECTIVITY
OF THE GRADER

1. ADAMS, W. L. "Why Teachers Say They Fail Pupils." *Educational Administration and Supervision,* 1932, 18, pp. 594-600
   What level of performance or behavior warrants a failing grade? Teachers responding to this investigation noted innumerable criteria ranging from such non-measurable points as "student shows no interest" or "not paying attention" to being absent too much of the time or not meeting certain specific academic standards. Specific criteria were rare, and the study revealed how arbitrary the factors underlying the failing grade really are. Yet, even though the criteria may be arbitrary and may change with time, the "failure" remains permanently on the student's record.

2. AIKEN, L. R. "The Grading Behavior of College Faculty." *Educational and Psychological Measurement,* 1963, 23, pp. 319-22
   This study revealed that although average SAT scores rose significantly for entering freshmen, there was no cor-

responding change in the grade averages of these entering students. (See the study by the University of California at Berkeley.)

3. BASS, B. M. "Intrauniversity Variation in Grading Practices." *Journal of Educational Psychology*, 1951, 42, pp. 366-68

It was discovered that grading was much more strict in the early college years and that standards differed dramatically among the various departments. (See Temple University study.)

4. BELLS, W. C. "Reliability of Repeated Grading of Essay Type Examinations." *Journal of Educational Psychology*, 1930, 21, pp. 48-52

Teachers, requested to regrade a series of geography and history examinations after a period of just less than three months, did so with generally poor reliability. (See Tieg study.)

5. COUSINS, GEORGE F. *et. al. Growth and Change at Indiana University, Vol. III—Teaching at Indiana University: Report of the Teaching Subcommittee of the University Study Committee*, Indiana University, 1966, in "Degrading Education," Center for Educational Reform, USNSA, 1969 (est.) p. 6

Cousins presents a side of the grading argument that has persisted over the past eighty years in spite of contradictory evidence. It is the assumption that teachers establish clearly defined educational objectives and criteria for their measurement. While it may be possible, it is not done and a high reliability coefficient is a rarity. (See Adams, Bells, Dexter, Engel, Odell, Tieg.) A statement from Cousins follows:

"With the increasing number of students in the University, and the difficulty resulting therefore from not getting to know a good many of the students well enough so that differentiated letters of recommendation can be written, it seems particularly important that we differentiate at least in grades as much as possible. Every faculty member knows that there is a great deal of difference between a B+ and a B−, or a C+ and a C−, even on the undergraduate level."

6. CRAWFORD, A. B. "Rubber Micrometers." *School and Society,* 1930, 32, pp. 223-40
This study of grades received by Yale University freshmen indicated that grades differed greatly according to departments, the experience of the staff and their expectations of how rapidly a new student should be expected to perform well.

7. DEXTER, E. S. "The Effect of Fatigue or Boredom on Teachers' Marks." *Journal of Educational Research,* 1935, 28, pp. 664-667
There is an endless variety of factors which might influence how a teacher marks one or a number of papers at any one point in time. Certainly one of the most obvious is the fatigue variable. Common sense is supported in this study which revealed that teachers respond to fatigue and time pressures in different ways. Some tend to become more lenient, while in other cases teachers become increasingly paricular. The problem of course, is that the conditions for fair grading seldom exist and more often than not teachers grade under pressures of time or personal fatigue.

8. EDWARDS, P. D. M. "The Use of Essays in Selection at 11 Plus: Essay Marking Experiments: Shorter and Longer Essays." Reported as part of a symposium in the *British Journal of Educational Psychology,* 1956, 26, pp. 128-36
The British have had more experience with developing

subjective essay-type examinations than anybody else and are well aware of the difficulty in grading them. Their School Certificate graders undergo intensive training in order to insure greater reliability. Even with this kind of practice, this study reports that examiners often disagree to a significant degree with each other and often are inconsistent in their grading procedures. It is little wonder that such inconsistencies are much worse when training is not required.

9. ENGLE, J. L. "Comparative Study of First and Final Marks." *School Review,* 1932, 40, pp. 61-66
Evidence in this study suggests there is a general pattern of consistency between grades given at the beginning of a term and at the end. This may be partly due to "self-fulfilling prophecies" on the part of students (poor students figure what's the use? and give up while better students are reinforced) or a self-fulfilling expectation on the part of the teacher. Also, it might be the result of certain teaching and testing methods selectively favoring some students. These are only a few of the possible explanations.

10. JOHNSON, FRANKLIN *The Administration and Supervision of a High School.* New York: Ginn, p. 402
In studying the determinants which went into their grading criteria, Johnson discovered no less than 49 different variables among the teachers investigated. (See also Odell)

11. KIRBY, B. C. "Three Error Sources in College Grades." *Journal of Experimental Education.* 1962, 31, pp. 213-18
The author reports that 206 lower division instructors at San Diego State College revealed a great discrepancy in the standards they used in grading. The median grade of these teachers ranged from below a C (1.82) to nearly an A (3.88). A similarly wide range was discovered among upper division instructors as well.

12. ODELL, C. W. "High School Marking Systems." *School Review*, 1925, 33, pp. 346-54

Not only do grades mean very different things to different teachers in a single school or university, but Odell found over one hundred different marking plans being used in the public high schools of one state, Illinois. Certainly the implications of this fact would be of great importance to employment or college admission officers. Thus, two five-point grading systems might be based on very different grading rationales.

13. PRESSEY, S. L. "Fundamental Misconceptions Involved in Current Marking Systems." *School and Society*, 1925, 21, pp. 736-8

A great many people, either explicitly or implicitly, use the concept of the normal curve when grading. This suggests that there tends to be a natural law of distribution along an imaginary line. (In the case of grades there is a distribution of probable errors.) If allowed to fall naturally along this imaginary line, performance would be patterned into five, seven or perhaps ten clusters. It is assumed that most would fall into a large central area with fewer at the extremes, thus resulting in a natural bell-shaped curve, indicative of the non-selectivity of the particular group. The proposals for which distribution pattern should be used in grading have been many but most of them involve five clusters (five-point grade system) including 3-24-46-24-3, 10-20-40-20-10, or even skewed distributions such as 15-33-33-15-4. In the first of these examples a teacher would attempt to restrict his grading so that 3% of the class would receive A's, 24% would receive B's, 46% would receive C's, 24% would receive D's and 3% would receive F's. While most teachers would not rigidly hold to such a scheme, many apparently have a general "normal curve rule-of-thumb" in mind when grading.

Pressey, as long as 45 years ago, stated that he believed much too much emphasis was being placed on the mathematical curve in determining acceptable levels of performance. He believed acceptable levels of performance should be specified instead through educational objectives which aim at helping every student reach them. If this were the case there could hardly be a normal distribution. One would hope that the successful teacher would have every student (if intellectually capable) receiving a passing or high grade. It is pointed out, however, that a "normal distribution" will not occur when students are homogeneously grouped, a test is too hard or too easy, a teacher is very effective or very ineffective, or, for a variety of reasons, students are highly motivated or not motivated at all. All too often the idea of the curve is indelibly imprinted on a teacher's mind, possibly influencing her entire approach to teaching and the student's approach to learning. (See also Smith and Wertz)

14. ROSENTHAL, R. and JACOBSEN, L. *Pygmalion in the Classroom: Self Fulfilling Prophecies and Teacher Expectations.* New York, Holt, Rinehart and Winston, 1969

If grades always represented an easily identified level of performance or merit, there might be some justification for them. The problem is that too many extraneous "other things" are brought into the process. In this case, the authors gave all the children in four California elementary schools an ordinary intelligence test at the beginning of the school year. The teachers were told that the tests were designed to reveal students who would probably show substantial IQ gains during the coming school year. Ten children were then selected *at random* from each class in the four schools and the teachers were informed that these ten children had done especially well on the test. Using these children as the experimental group and all of the other children as the controls, an intelligence test given at the end of the year revealed that the children in the experimental groups in the kindergarten, first, second and third grades made significant gains in IQ when compared with the children in the control groups. Also, the teachers tended to rate the experimental group children higher in such areas as cooperativeness, interest, school affairs and social adjustment. The teachers' expectations contributed to these differences. The perceived results of the first test scores stimulated behaviors on the part of the teachers, and eventually on the part of the "favored" students, thus resulting in the performance discrepancy. Again, the problem is that in another situation, the stimulus might come from word of mouth (another teacher), a look at last year's report card, the color of a student's skin or even the clothes he wears. It might be from language or a teacher having observed the parents of a child. Who is to say what all the variables are which are impinging on the teacher's set? And to what degree are these influencing the grading process as well?

15. ROTHNEY, W. M. JOHN *Evaluating and Reporting Pupil Progress,* Washington, D. C. National Education Association, 1955, p. 13

Rothney takes a hard look at testing practices and their influence in the counseling process. "The so-called 'objective test' is really a subjectively constructed test that is objectively scored. The actual writing of the test items is a subjective process. The author of an objectively scored test must decide on the materials he will sample, must make judgment about whether or not an item is worthy of inclusion, and must select among scoring schemes . . . no objective scoring system can ever make up for faulty subjective decisions made during the construction of the test."

16. SIMS, V. M. "Reducing the Variability of Essay Examination Marks Through the Eliminating of Variation in Standards of Grading." *Journal of Educational Research,* 1932, 26, pp. 637-47

This article suggests clear, rational ways of improving grading efficiency. Many of these had been suggested earlier, and many teachers are aware of them even today. The problem is that they are seldom put into practice because they require additional time in scoring or because they assume too many constraints on the teacher.

17. SMITH, O. M. "Grading Without Guesswork." *Educational Psychology Measurement,* 1953, 13, pp. 367-90

In an attempt to answer the criticisms relating to grading procedures and including those directed at the "normal distribution" approach to grading, Smith suggested a variety of approaches so that the normal curve could be adapted more easily by teachers. His effort was designed to make the teacher aware of the limitations and the strengths of this approach and to provide practical suggestions.

18. STARCH, DANIEL and ELLIOTT, EDWARD C. "Reliability of the Grading of High School Work in English." *School Review,* 1912, 20, pp. 442-57

19. ———. "Reliability of Grading Work in Mathematics." *School Review,* 1913, 21, pp. 254-95

20. ———. "Reliability of Grading Work in History." *School Review,* 1913, 21, pp. 676-81

In three simply designed studies the authors desired to determine the degree to which the grading standards of teachers were influenced by their own personal values and expectations. Thus, for example, by taking a single high school geometry paper and having copies sent to 180 teachers to be graded on the basis of 100 points, with 75 being a passing mark, comparisons could be made in terms of actual scores and criteria among all the responding teachers. What this research team found shook the roots of the educational world. In each of the subject areas the grades submitted (approximately 75% response) ranged from one end of the grading scale of the other. In the first experiment (English) a range of 39 points was found. Critics of the experiment, however, argued that there were too many subjective elements to expect high reliability. They suggested that the authors try something more concrete, like mathematics or science. This they did and to their astonishment an even wider range of scores was produced. In grading the geometry paper two teachers scored the paper in the 38-42 range, and eight teachers scored it in the 83-87 range. Instead of greater reliability, there was even less. The more concrete, objective subject matter seemed even more vulnerable to varying standards than either English or history. It was found that some teachers marked off for neatness, organization, and not showing calculations. Others gave points for partially correct responses or didn't mark off if the method was correct and the actual answer slightly wrong. The variables were innumerable. Most important, it was discovered in each of the three areas that the variability in marks is not a function of the subject, but rather it appears to be a function of the grader and the method of the examination. These experiments were a landmark in casting doubt upon the reliability of testing and grading procedures.

21. Temple University, *Report of the College of Education Ad Hoc Committee on Grading Systems*, 1968, pp. 41-48
Studies at Temple University corroberated investigations at other universities. There was found to be a large variability

in grades distributed in different colleges in the University. Similarly, grades differed dramatically between departments in the same colleges and among faculty in the same department or college. For example, in a beginning course in the College of Education, 82% of the 385 students taking the course were given *A* or *B* grades. Only 2% received a *D* or *F* grade. On the other hand, in the College of Liberal Arts over 30% received a *D* or *F* grade in a similar introductory course. The two colleges (at least the departments responsible for these courses) have very different grading standards. But, even more striking is the variance in grades of different professors teaching the same course. The following example appears to be representative of many which could have been drawn from this report.

Course X enrolled 514 students (students were randomly sectioned within a range of certain time demands of the students) in an introductory course within the College of Liberal Arts. Taking all of the sections together, 32% of the students received *A* or *B* grades and 37% received *D* or *F* grades. An interesting comparison can be made, however, between the grades distributed in Instructor Y's section and those distributed in Instructor Z's section.

	No. of A's	No. of B's	No. of C's	No. of D's	No. of F's
Course X N = 514	57 = 11%	106 = 20.6%	151 = 29.3%	113 = 21.9%	87 = 17%
Section Y N = 34	0 = 0%	1 = 2.9%	10 = 29.4%	7 = 20.5%	16 = 47%
Section Z N = 30	7 = 23.3%	9 = 30%	12 = 40%	2 = 6.6%	0 = 0%

Thus, if a student by chance drew Instructor Y for his course, he found himself in the most demanding section with virtually no chance of receiving an *A* or *B* grade. Two-thirds of these students could expect a less than satisfactory grade. In contrast, Instructor Z's students could reasonably expect to receive a satisfactory grade (80%). There is little doubt that the two instructors were using very different grading standards and very likely different procedures. In real terms as far as the student is concerned, it could mean the difference between probation and failure or between the Dean's List and no recognition. This example could be repeated many times in the same institution and hundreds of times over throughout the country. The question is not whether grading systems can be more equitable or more reliable. The fact is that grades are not reliable nor are they valid indications of a student's level of performance. Since this pattern has not changed in the last half century, it may suggest that changes should be considered until practices are in line with grading objectives.

22. THOMPSON, W. N. "A Study of the Grading Practices of 31 Instructors in Freshman English." *Journal of Educational Measurement*, 1955, 49, pp. 65-8

Studying the grades of 31 instructors in an English composition course resulted in the discovery that mean grades varied from 3.02 to 4.20 (5-pt. system) Again, this study revealed the degree to which standards of grading may differ among teachers of the same course in the same college.

23. TIEG, E. W. "Educational Diagnosis." (Monterey, California: California Testing Bureau) Educational Bulletin #18, 1952

A good example of the inability of teachers to be consistent in re-marking papers as soon as two months after the initial grading. In this experiment ten examinations were regarded by the same teacher, based on a 100-point marking scale.

Pupil No.	First Marking	Second Marking
1	85	70
2	50	75
3	90	95

4	90	85
5	90	70
6	99	90
7	70	60
8	75	80
9	60	80
10	90	75

On the first marking the teacher had a classroom distribution with a mean of 80 points and on the second grading a mean of 78. The problem was that every paper averaged a 14-point change, either up or down the grading scale. Thus, one student who probably failed the first test with a 60 scored an 80 on the second, and another student who scored 90 on the first paper scored only a 70 on the second. While not representative of a rigorous experiment, this example could undoubtedly be replicated a thousand times by teachers in the field.

24. University of California at Berkeley, *Report on Methods of Evaluating Students at the University of California— Berkeley,* October, 1965, p. 13

One of the important findings of this broadly based study involved the fact that students seemed to be graded with quite different criteria by their teachers, both in high school and college. Also, whether or not students as a whole have improved academically in terms of knowledge, their grades have changed little. While one would expect better performance to be revealed in higher grades, this did not occur in this study. The following chart relates to the freshmen who matriculated on the University of California Campus at Berkeley between the years 1947 and 1960. (See Pressey note)

	Verbal SAT	Math. SAT	H.S. GPA	U.C. GPA
Male (1947)	491	508	3.32	2.34
Male (1960)	557	595	3.45	2.34
Female (1947)	483	411	3.40	2.34
Female (1960)	543	518	3.51	2.34

While SAT scores jumped anywhere from 50 to over 100 points during this period of time and entering high school grades improved somewhat, the average grades received at the University did not improve. Taking only the scores of the male students entering the University, it is to be noted that during the same period of time that their performance on the SAT in math increased 15% and on the SAT Verbal increased 12%, their high school grades only increased 4%. In other words, there was little apparent recognition in their own high schools of the changing performance standards. This is particularly discouraging for a student in one school who does good work but receives only average (grade) recognition, while a student from another school who is equal in ability receives an excellent grade. If both these students apply to the same school and have similar SAT scores, there is little doubt which will be chosen if a choice must be made. Similarly, at Berkeley the grades have gone virtually unchanged over the thirteen-year period of the study. One questions whether grading is being done on the basis of excellence. Either this is not the case or there is a dramatic decrease in the level of student motivation during this period at the University.

25. WETZEL, WILLIA "The Use of the Normal Curve of Distribution in Estimating Student Marks." *School Review*, 1929, 29

This study presents a general exploratory study of the uses of the normal curve in the grading process at a period of time when it was a central point in educational discussion.

II. GRADES AND THEIR RELATIONSHIP TO
NON-INTELLECTUAL VARIABLES
(Motivation, Anxiety, Creativity, Conformity, Cheating)

26. ABORN, M. "The Influence of Experimentally Induced Failure on the Retention of Material Acquired Through Set and Instrumental Learning." *Journal of Experimental Psychology,* 1953, 45, pp. 225-31

It is very difficult to determine whether grades, in themselves, actually pose enough of a threat to some students to warrant their removal. For ethical reasons it is difficult to create high anxiety conditions within the schools and to test what might be parallel conditions to the grading process. This study is representative of many in the field and uses a laboratory design and method. While supporting much educational theory, the findings are difficult to generalize to actual practice. The major finding of the study is that individuals under a condition that is perceived as threatening to them will remember less information than when the threatening condition is removed.

27. BAKER, R. L. and DOYLE, R. P. "A Change in Marking Procedures and Scholastic Achievement." *Educational Administration and Supervision,* 1957, 4, pp. 223-32

This study explored the degree to which the individual reporting of grades rather than the more traditional "report card method" would induce an improvement in academic achievement. It was found that achievement did not improve. This study is typical of many whose results are used to actually support the maintenance of grades and should be looked at more carefully. An assumption underlying the study, or at least its interpretation, is that grades should be a stimulant to performance. Little was done to report the feelings of the students in relation to the change or whether the intervention was helpful in bringing parents a clearer understanding of grading, or whether, in fact, lines of communication were opened between the home and the school because of the nature of the feedback process with the child. The humanizing of a school cannot be quantified in terms of the achievement dimension alone. The problem is that the report of these findings might be enough to halt the experimental program, even though over a long period of time the actual learning environment might be influenced in a positive manner. Often the researcher is after immediate significant changes which should not be expected as part of a cumulative process.

28. BOSTROM, R. N., VLANDIS, J. W. and ROSENBAUM, M. E. "Grades as Reinforcing Contingencies and Attitude Change." *Journal of Educational Psychology,* 1961, 52, pp. 112-115

The question is often asked whether or not grades lead students into a pattern of academic conformity? This contention was supported in this study which revealed that students receiving *A* grades when they expressed ideas contrary to previously stated beliefs tended to shift their beliefs in this same direction more than students in the experiment who received *D* grades for their non-divergent views. Teacher support was clearly a factor in the move toward the new value position. In this case support could be equated with a high grade.

29. BOWERS, WILLIAM. *Student Dishonesty and its Control in College,* New York: Bureau of Applied Behavioral Science, 1964 appeared in: Becker, Howard, *et. al. Making the Grade: The Academic Side of College Life,* New York: John Wiley and Sons, 1968 (?), pp. 101-102

In a national survey it was reported that at least 50% of the responding students admitted having cheated during college in the form of plagarizing, using crib notes, copying on an examination or turning in someone else's examination paper. The author summarized his research on grades by saying: "The most important point about illegitimate actions is that they are a consequence of a system of examinations and grade points . . . Illegitimate actions would be foolish if nothing important could be gained from them. It is because they may be rewarded by a raised grade that students engage in them."

30. BRIM, O. G. JR., GOSLIN, D. A., GLASS, D. C. and GOLDBERG, I. *The Use of Standardized Ability Tests in American Secondary Schools,* New York: Russell Sage Foundation, 1964.

The authors believe that variables, such as school grades and acceptance by peers have a much greater impact on the shaping of one's estimate of his own ability than the scores he receives on tests. While the book has considerable rigorous documentation, it falls short in the attempt to separate the "reporting process" from the notion of testing and evaluation. The two must be perceived as part of the same package.

31. CALDWELL, E. and HARNETT, R. "Sex Biases in College Grading." *Journal of Educational Measurement,* 1967, 4, pp. 129-32

Taking a sample of men and women from 167 course sections over six different introductory courses, the investigators compared male and female grades obtained from the course instructors. It was discovered that even when controlling for past achievement and a number of other variables, females tended to receive higher grades than would have been expected based on performance alone. While it was difficult to separate the kinds of biases involved, it was clear that the differences were not the result of such factors as maturity.

32. CARTER, R. S. "How Invalid Are Marks Assigned By Teachers?" *Journal of Educational Psychology,* 1952, 43, pp. 218-28

Fifteen years prior to Caldwell's study, Carter found very similar results with a non-college population. He was able to control for both achievement and intellectual ability and found that there was a consistent tendency for teachers to reward girls with higher grades than boys.

33. CHILD, I. L. and WHITING. "Determinants of Level of Aspiration: Evidence from Everyday Life." *Journal of Abnormal Psychology* 1949, 44, pp. 303-14

The conclusions of these and other well-known researchers are:

1. That success leads to rising levels of aspiration and failure leads to more unrealistic levels of aspiration—usually too low, but sometimes too high (perhaps an over-compensation);

2. That the stronger the level of success experienced by the individual, the greater his increased level of expectation and the greater his chances of achieving this level of aspiration;

3. That a shift in a student's level of aspiration usually signifies a change in his confidence level in achieving his goal;

4. That perceived failure will usually lead to a withdrawal from goal-seeking behavior which leads to new failure.

The problem is that educational systems revolve around reward and failure as received through grades. Those students who need the encouragement the most and need to be involved to the highest degree are the very ones experiencing failure through grades. Occasional failure is not bad, but a destructive cycle as suggested here is.

34. EDMISTON, R. W. "Do Teachers Show Partiality Toward Boys or Girls?" *Peabody Journal of Education*, 1943, 20, pp. 234-38

This study indicates that boys will tend to receive generally lower grades than girls when IQ and past achievement are controlled. In addition to this, it was discovered that female teachers have a tendency to give higher grades to the girls than the male teachers although male teachers also give higher grades than would be expected. It is possible that teachers are responding to a tendency for girls to internalize "school values" more quickly than boys, yet it is not easily determined. It is clear that irrelevant variables outside the stated grading criteria are helping to determine grades for these children.

35. FALA, MICHAEL A. *Dunce Cages, Hickory Sticks, and Public Evaluations: The Structure of Academic Authoritarianism,* The Teaching Assistant Association, University of Wisconsin, 1968, pp. 11 & 12

Reporting data gathered by the Bureau of Applied Social Research at Columbia University, Fala noted that at least half of the 5000 students interviewed admitted to cheating. The indication was that the incidents of cheating were highest among weak students, men, career-oriented majors and those in school because of other than academic interest (sports, music, etc.). Fala sounded a discouraging note in his summary: "We are faced with the inescapable fact that any time we receive a set of term papers, a substantial proportion of them will be the product of one of the numerous intra- or inter-campus term paper rings which, to those interested in criminal syndicalism and white collar crime, are among the more fascinating and exotic of the innovative adoptions of students."

36. FOX, ROBERT; LIPPITT, RONALD; and SCHMUCK, RICHARD.

Pupil-Teacher Adjustment and Mutual Adaptation in Creating Classroom Learning Environments. U.S. Department of Health, Education and Welfare, Office of Education, Cooperative Research Project #1167, Ann Arbor: University of Michigan, 1964

This research team found that those students who are liked by their peers tend to have good feelings about themselves and tend to utilize their own intellectual capabilities more than students of low peer status. Similarly, it was found that students liked by the teacher were less isolated in the class and had a more positive image of themselves (high self-esteem). Students who found themselves more isolated from the teacher (less liked) tended to have a less positive image of the school. For boys and girls combined, satisfaction with the teacher and utilization of intelligence were found to be associated when the effects of social class, parental support and peer status were held constant. (See Jung et al.)

37. GOLDBERG, MIRIAM L., PARSONS, HARRY and JUSTMAN, JOSEPH *The Effects of Ability Grouping.* New York: Teachers College Press (Columbia University), 1966
The studies of these authors suggest unequivocally that ability grouping has no important effect on academic achievement. They raise the disturbing possibility that instead of actually resulting in more individualized instruction, ability grouping may lead to what they call "selective deprivation."

38. HOLLAND, J. L. "Prediction of College Grades from Personality and Aptitude Variables." *Journal of Educational Psychology* 1960, 51, pp. 245-54
This study suggests that personality traits which describe individuals characterized as "creative" tend to be significantly different from the traits recognized in "achievers."

Thus, the highly grade-conscious achiever tends to be less willing to take risks, more subject to group standards and pressures, less dominating, more persistent and has a stronger superego, among other things. The question, of course, is what type of student are we trying to develop in our schools; and are grades, in fact, not restricting what appears to be acceptable behavior?

39. JUNG, CHARLES C., FOX, ROBERT and LIPPITT, RONALD "An Orientation and Strategy for Working on Problems of Change in School Systems." in *Change in School Systems* (G. Watson ed.) Published for Cooperative Project for Educational Development by National Training Laboratories, NEA, Washington, D. C., 1967, pp. 68-88
Articles in this section by Fox, et. al., Lippitt, and Schmuck and Van Edmond are quoted as part of an analysis focusing on various aspects of research utilization and the implementation of planned change programs in school systems.

40. KELLEY, E. G. "A Study of Consistent Discrepancies Between Instructor Grades and Test Results." *Journal of Educational Psychology,* 1958, 49, pp. 328-34
This study supports the previously cited investigation by Holland. Kelley found certain types of personality characteristics present in high achieving students when compared to lower achieving peers.

41. KNOWLTON, JAMES Q. and HAMERLYNCK, LEO *Journal of Educational Psychology,* December, 1967, pp. 379-85
No fewer than 81% of the students involved in this study admitted cheating in college, and 46% indicated that they had cheated that very semester. At least 40% said they cheated in some form or another rather regularly. This is particularly interesting since the population for the study was drawn from both rural and urban universities. (See: items for Bowers and for Fala.) Such information throws

serious doubt on the validity of the grading process as it now exists in our universities and colleges.

42. KURTZ, J. J. and SWENSON, E. J. "Factors Related to Over-Achievement and Under-Achievement in School." *School Review,* 1951, 59, pp. 472-80

The authors attempted to determine whether students working under a "normal curve" approach to grading (so many *A*'s, *B*'s, *C*'s etc. allocated each grading period) or students under a system that allowed grades to be distributed according to relative performance and improvement would reveal greater motivation. The level of student aspiration and actual academic improvement was significantly greater in the group not restricted by a predetermined curve.

43. LENTZ, T. J. "Sex Differences in School Marks with Achievement Scores Constant." *School and Society,* 1929, 29, pp. 65-68

Girls are often perceived by teachers as being higher achievers than boys of the same age, particularly in the early grades where earlier maturity of girls is suggested as an important variable. This was not found to be the case by Lentz who gave nearly 400 boys and girls in grades 2 to 6 a standardized achievement test. Contrary to expectation, the boys scored a full 8% higher than the girls. However, revealing what a large part teacher expectations (knowingly or unknowingly) play in the grading process, it was discovered that the teachers graded the girls 8% higher than they did the higher achieving boys.

44. LEVINE, M., WESOLOWSKI, J. and CORBETT, F. "Pupil Turnover and Academic Performance in an Inner City Elementary School." *Psychology in The Schools,* 1966, 3, pp. 153-58

The psychological stress and tensions that accompany a student when transferring from one school to another can be great. This study revealed that students are handicapped in their academic achievement because of movement under such conditions from one school to another. Some students are subject to such changes a number of times in a single year.

45. LIPPITT, RONALD "Unplanned Maintenance and Planned Change in the Group Work Process." *Social Work Practice,* New York: Columbia University Press, 1962, (See Jung *et al.*)

Whether or not grades influence the teaching-learning equation has been debated for years. This report by Lippitt stated: "We find, for example, in an average elementary school class, that the majority of the pupils perceive that most of the other pupils are against too active cooperation with the teachers, are against being 'eager beavers' about study and learning. Nevertheless, the majority of the group, in confidence, will indicate a great desire to be more active, to be more involved, yet there is a collusion to maintain mutual ignorance." Certainly this provides one sure way of maintaining at least a minimal level of safety in a threatening environment which is governed by the stigma of constant evaluation.

46. MANEY, C. A. "Sex Bias in College Marking." *Journal of Higher Education,* 1933, 4, pp. 29-31

A ten year study of grading at Transylvania College was directed at discovering the variations in grades given men and women students. The author concluded that there was a definite sex bias found which favored women in the college over men.

47. MARSHALL, M. "Self Evaluation in Seventh Grade." *Elementary School Journal,* 1960, 60, pp. 249-52

Students were asked to grade their own work twice a month in terms of satisfactory, good and poor. These were discussed with their teachers. Each student was given help in determining and understanding his own grading criteria. Marshall found that the students tended to become more involved in their work and interested in their progress as they became more accountable to themselves. In addition, parents seemed better able to accept the evaluation of the teacher at the end of the term since this was based in part on the child's own estimate of his performance.

48. MILLER, STUART *Measure, Number, and Weight: A Polemical Statement of the College Grading Problem.* Center of Research on Learning and Teaching, The University of Michigan, Ann Arbor, 1967, pp. 20-21

In this document the author covers the broad spectrum of grading issues and challenges the universities to explore new alternatives to the grading process. Miller gathered much of his information as a result of the comprehensive study of grading at the University of California at Berkeley (See: Sect. I, Univ. of California). At one point he stresses the low correlation between grades and creativity and says: "It seems clear that the grading system, at all levels including the graduate one, tends to reward the conforming plodder and to penalize the imaginative student who is likely to make a significant contribution to nearly any field. It is obvious that the discouragement and neglect that creative students tend to receive are only expressed in grades. The causes of the problem . . . lie deeper within our education structure."

Miller's monograph is full of pertinent research and challenging polemic on grading, and the authors recommend it highly.

49. PAGE, E. B. "Teacher Comments and Student Performance." *Journal of Educational Psychology,* 49, 1958, pp. 173-81

In this study of 74 high school classrooms, each teacher administered an objective test, one that would normally occur as part of the class evaluation. Then the papers were sorted randomly into three different groups. In the first group, student papers were given no comment along with their grades. In a second group, grades were accompanied with whatever comments appeared to the teachers to be relevant and helpful to the child. In the third group, a particular grade was given a very specific comment. For example, all *A* papers might receive "Excellent, keep it up!" or an *F* paper might receive "Let's raise that grade!" The next time an objective test was given, the three groups were compared to determine if any one stimulus (no comment, free comments, restricted comments) produced the greatest response on the part of students in terms of performance. The free comment papers, where teachers responded naturally, showed the greatest improvement to a significant degree over the no comment papers. Again and again it is shown that the human variable is the greatest motivator, yet the grade remains the center of most evaluation reports.

50. PHILLIPS, BEEMAN "Sex, Social Class and Anxiety as Sources of Variation in School Anxiety." *Journal of Educational Psychology,* 1962, 53, pp. 316-22
This study indicated that anxiety lowered grades of middle ability students while an anxiety producing condition actually increased the grades of high ability students. This is to say both groups were anxious, one group was simply able to mobilize its resources under stress better than the other. Again, those who might "need" success the most are least able to achieve it.

51. PHILLIPS, BEEMAN "The Classroom: A Place to Learn" in CLARK, D. H. and LESSER, GERALD S. (editors) *Emotional Disturbance and School Learning,* Chicago: Science

Research Associates, 1965, pp. 263-4

A summary of important research findings in the area of classroom anxiety presented by Phillips suggested that highly anxious students seem to perform better under neutral conditions. But less anxious students seem to perform more effectively under ego involving conditions. Research also suggests that lower-class males have less ego involvement and less debilitating anxiety in the classroom than more ego involved students with a high personal (or family) investment in the game of learning. One is not certain whether this lack of ego involvement by lower-class males is the result of the classroom simply being irrelevant to their needs or whether it is a defense mechanism for handling the anxiety created in a competitive learning environment with the more overtly anxious achievers.

52. RYAN, F. R. and DAVIE, J. S. "Social Acceptance, Academic Achievement, and Aptitude Among High School Students." *Journal of Educational Research*, 1958, 52, pp. 101-106

The authors found popularity was not to any significant degree (except among junior boys) related to academic achievement (grades) in the four classes studied. This might be anticipated since students associate with whom they feel comfortable and are accepted. Thus, popularity is relative to a particular group . . . except in the case of a very few students which would not alter the results. However, one might hypothesize that grades would be a factor in the various friendship groups, if these were isolated. Interestingly enough, the authors found no relationship between grades and student associations (See: Fox; Schmuck)

53. SHAW, M. C. and McCUEN, J. T. "The Onset of Academic Under-Achievement in Bright Children." *Journal of*

Educational Psychology, 1960, 51, pp. 103-108

A wide range of variables are explored in this study which seem to influence the beginning of poor achievement by previously successful students. A point well taken is that a student achieving success will rarely lose interest or motivation unless he is impacted by a traumatic experience. A child who is achieving poorly is not so certain of continuing poor performance, although it is clear that failure usually leads to withdrawal or acting out behaviors, and this cycle becomes self-generating and very difficult to break. An academic-graded system requires performance for success. Many failing students are not capable of achieving under emotional stress. It is difficult to provide alternative rewards when the grade is perceived as the one legitimate reward of the system.

54. SCHMUCK, RICHARD, and VAN EGMOND, ELMER "Sex Differences in the Relationship of Interpersonal Perceptions to Academic Performance." *Psychology in the Schools,* 1965, 2, pp. 32-40

The authors stress the critical relationship of the teacher to the student as a factor in student performance. It was found that the students who had the closest relationships to the teacher (seen as most compatible) achieved greater academic success than did students who appeared less compatible. Since the teacher is the source of rewards based on academic as well as emotional criteria, and the two are admittedly difficult to separate, a student failing academically may, in fact, be reflecting a social problem as much as an academic one. Yet the grade remains.

55. WRINKLE, W. L. *Improving Marking and Reporting Practices in Elementary and Secondary Schools.* New York: Rinehart and Co., 1950

Many see grades as motivating students to work, as well as

mobilizing their efforts to specific tasks and building within them a needed work ethic for being successful in a competitive society. Others see this as falacious and believe that grades hold no parallel in the adult world with its work and incentive system. Wrinkle for one sees education as having failed to define its objectives as clearly as industry, and thus most graded evaluations are subjective and lack the motivating influence they might have if the goals were explicitly stated and were measurable. For too many, grades are seen as the end product of the educational process.

III. GRADES AS PREDICTORS OF ACADEMIC AND OCCUPATIONAL PERFORMANCE

56. ANDERSON, J. J. "Correlation Between Academic Achievement and Teaching Success." *Elementary School Journal,* 1931, 32, pp. 22-9
Ratings of on-the-job performance of 590 Northern State Teacher College graduates by their school superintendents or principals correlated only .12 with high school grades and .19 with college grade-point average. In spite of this and other evidence, colleges of education continue to have specific cutoff points for entrance into their professional program, and employers use the point-grade as an important criterion in selection.

57. BARR, A. S. *et al., Wisconsin Studies of the Measurement and Predication of Teacher Effectiveness,* Madison: Dembar Publications, 1961
In this summary of thirty-three studies, supervisor ratings were found to have a median correlation of .09 with the college grade-point averages of the teachers. This suggests that well over 90% of the variance which explains teaching success is determined by other variables.

58. BRECKENRIDGE, ELIZABETH "A Study of the Relation of Preparatory School Records and Intelligence Test Scores to Teaching Success." *Educational Administration and Supervision,* 1932, 18

A slightly higher relationship exists between college grades and supervisors' ratings of teachers (.35) and their teaching performance. Still, the relationship is surprisingly low. It is most interesting that the teacher is constantly in the position of grading performance which eventually influences a person's range of job opportunities. But, if grades are used as a major criterion in teacher selection, a great injustice is being done to the teacher.

59. CARLILE, A. B. "Predicting Performance in the Teaching Profession." *Journal of Educational Research,* 67, pp. 38-45

The author related student teaching grades to a wide range of variables (used 16 different tests to obtain scores) including intelligence, teaching aptitude, scholastic achievement, proficiency in basic skills and personality traits. Only low positive relationships were found between student teaching grades and these other variables, except for the relationship between student teaching grades and scholastic achievement. This relatively high correlation (.46) suggests that the student was most adept at playing the "grading game" in college. Thus, the correlation between the student's teaching ability and his overall college grades was greater than that between his teaching ability and his grade for student teaching. According to this, the criteria used to test excellence in the student teaching course were very different from those required on the teaching job.

60. *College Student Profiles,* Iowa City: American College Testing Program, 1966, pp. 19-20

One explanation why there is a tendency for college grades

not to be good predictors of occupational success is that although colleges and universities differ greatly in their own selection and academic standards, it was found in this study that grade distributions are almost identical. Thus, in four hundred schools studied, representing all degrees of selectivity, the distribution of *A*'s, *B*'s, *C*'s etc. appeared to be the same.

61. GOSLIN, D. A. "Standardized Ability Tests and Testing." *Science,* Feb. 1968, pp. 851-55

The author refers to Terman's famous studies of intellectually gifted children which indicated that although the gifted children as a group were more successful than a less gifted group, he found no relationship between intelligence and later performance within the members of the gifted group.

   (See: TERMAN, L. M. *The Gifted Group at Mid-Life,* Stanford University Press, 1959)

Goslin concluded from this and his own studies that intellectual abilities may function as a threshold variable in relation to occupational advancement, but once at or above this threshold, one's success among his peers in the same field will depend on non-intellectual variables not measured by intelligence tests, grades or other cognitive factors.

62. HILLS, J. R. "Predictions of College Grades for all Public Colleges of a State." *Journal of Educational Measurement,* 1964, 1, pp. 155-9

This study seems representative of the findings of many researchers who have explored the relationship between college achievement as measured by grades and by high school rank. Hills' investigation is based on a population of approximately 28,000 students. He found correlations ranging from .54 to .57 between these two variables, and when he combined high school rank with the two Scholastic Aptitude Tests (Verbal and Mechanical), he found a multiple correlation of .64.

63. HILLS, J. R., KLOCK, J. A. and BUSH, M. "The Use of Academic Predication Equations with Subsequent Classes." *American Educational Research Journal,* 1965, 2, pp. 203-206

The authors discovered that grades in one year can be used with considerable efficiency when predicting grades in subsequent years. Thus, a correlation of over .60 could be expected between a GPA obtained in one year and one predicted in another year. Again, there is no doubt that grades are relatively efficient predictors of future grades.

64. HOYT, P. DONALD *The Relationship Between College Grades and Adult Achievement,* ACT Research Report No. 7, Iowa City: American College Testing Program, 1965

This extensive study and summary of 46 research studies suggests that there is virtually no positive correlation between grades in college and future success in the real world of work outside of academia. Grades just do not seem to be valid predictors of future accomplishment in the great majority of cases.

65. KAPPELL, F. R. *From the World of College to the World of Work,* New York: American Telephone and Telegraph Co., 1962

Research from the American Telephone and Telegraph Co. revealed a slight positive correlation between college grades and final salaries attained by organization employees. There were not found to be positive correlations in terms of other performance criteria. (Reported in Miller, Section II)

66. KLUGH, H. E. and BIERLEY, R. "The School and College Ability Test and High School Grades as Predictors of Achievement." *Educational and Psychological Measure-*

ment, 1959, 19, pp. 625-26

This research supported other studies in the field which show the relatively high correlation between high school rank (HSR) and college grades. In this case the correlation was over .60, and by adding the SCAT test, the multiple correlation rose to over .66.

67. LAVIN, D. E. *The Prediction of Academic Performance,* New York: The Russell Sage Foundation, 1965

The author, having explored much of the literature in the field, suggests that it is important to note that the highest correlations between test scores and grades and subsequent achievement are obtained in the short run. The longer the time between the test and the criterion measure, the less is the magnitude of the correlation. The fact remains that test scores correlate only moderately with long-range academic performance and not at all with post-academic performance. Also, a problem of range restriction occurs as one climbs the academic ladder. Thus, students leaving college have already gone through a number of selection screens based on much more than grades. Grades lose their potency as a predictor as the group becomes increasingly homogeneous in relation to grades. For this reason grades and aptitude tests make poor predictors of graduate school success and of job performance since it is the other variables that will make the difference at this point in the selection process.

68. LEWIS, W. A. "Early Prediction of College GPA Using Precollege Grades." *Journal of Educational Measurement,* 1966, 3, pp. 35-36

Lewis found that achievement in terms of grades received in the early years of elementary school correlated at a low level with later grades in college (.00 to .30). He found a correlation between high school and college grades of around .50 depending on the particular year.

69. MARASCULLO, L. A. and GILL, G. "Measurable Differences Between Successful and Unsuccessful Doctoral Candidates in Education." *California Journal of Educational Research,* 1967, 18, pp. 65-70

A recent study found very few of the traditional academic variables to differentiate between successful and unsuccessful doctoral students. In fact, the only variable · that significantly differentiated among them was a commitment to do scholarly work. Interestingly enough, undergraduate GPA did not act as a discriminating factor among the candidates.

70. MARTIN, R. A. and PACHERES, J. "Good Scholars Not Always the Best." cited in *Business Week,* Feb. 24, 1962, pp. 77-78

Even in the highly specific skill fields such as engineering, there is little relationship between grades and eventual success. In this study there was not even a relationship found between grades and on-the-job salaries. (See: Kappel, Section III)

71. PALLETT, J. B. *Definition and Predictions of Success in the Business World,* Unpublished Doctoral Dissertation, University of Iowa, 1965

Eight characteristics of job success were defined by the author, and he found no positive relationships between these distinct characteristics as rated by supervisors and the grades received in college by the experimental population.

72. PRINCE, P. B., TAYLOR, C. W., RICHARDS, J. M., JR. and JACOBSEN, T. L. *Performance Measures of Physicians.* Final report submitted to the United States Office of Education, Washington, D. C., 1963, reported in: *Degrading Education,* Center for Educational Reform, USNSA, 1969

Although grades in medical school have been shown to have

a slight relationship to early success in the field, over the long run, no relationship was found between medical school grades and a list of twenty-four performance characteristics of physicians. A slight relationship was found between grades and those doctors who contributed to the professional literature.

73. REICHSTEIN, KENNETH J. and PIPKIN, RONALD M. "A Study of Academic Justice." *The Law and Society Review,* 1968, Vol. 2, #2

Reichstein and Pipkin explored the use of grades in the decision of an appeals body at the University of Wisconsin. Students (numbering 200) who desired to appeal an earlier decision of academic probation or expulsion at the University were each given approximately thirty minutes before the Appeals Board. They found, for example, that students with low college grades caused the Board to look into the high school GPA of the student. In the case of one student, a Board member stated: "She had three *F*'s. If she had one *F*, I would have let her stay." It is this kind of mentality that makes the grade a dangerous weapon in the hands of many people. In this case it was in the hands of the academic deans and faculty members who made up the Appeals Board. In another case a Board member stated: "———— was a fairly bright boy but he had a weird personal appearance—a Beatle haircut. He said he wanted an understanding of his personality, but he placed it on a personal basis. We all agreed that he had a bad record."

How totally biasing this kind of language is. In the case of this individual, he had a cumulative GPA of 1.80 and a semester GPA of 1.92. The Board is talking about a boy's future in relation to tenths of points and in terms of personal characteristics which have nothing to do with performance, although, as seen previously (Sect. II), they often influence grading standards. This Board is using the grade as an absolute measure, and it reflects the power of that grade at a point of greatest stress in the life of any student. Finally, 'grades may well be able to predict future grades with a large number of students. But, in the case of any individual there are too many unpredictable variables to place much weight on this factor. After all, the student facing the Board did pass the school's entrance screening and was perceived as academically capable.

74. TRAXLER, A. E. "A Study of the Junior Scholastic Aptitude Test." *Journal of Educational Research,* 1941, 35, pp. 16-27
Many studies have been conducted which reveal a positive correlation between various aptitude tests and achievement. Thus, for example, in this study numerical aptitude as measured on the Junior Scholastic Aptitude Test correlated .59 with mathematics grades (slightly less than predictable from previous math grades) and a surprisingly high .52 with grades in English. This is interesting since verbal aptitude correlated only .55 with English. A point to be made here is that with the availability of multiple correlational techniques, it is possible to develop batteries of measures for predicting future academic success without necessarily using GPA or HSR and still be assured of nearly as good results as one would have with the more traditional predictors.

75. WRIGHT, PATRICIA S. *Enrollment for Advanced Degrees* ( )E-5401-63, Circular No. 786. Washington, D. C. Office of Education, U.S. Department of Health, Education and Welfare, 1965. Reported in: Miller, Stuart (Section II.) There is evidence that there is an extraordinarily high attrition rate in graduate schools among those students seeking the Ph.D. One government estimate is that the

rate of attrition is close to 20 to 1. That is, for every student who actually receives the degree from the university, twenty will fail to complete their program. Even if this figure is grossly inaccurate, it can be stated that selective procedures with grades as the keystone in the process are ineffective. It is the non-intellectual factors that are of greatest influence at this advanced level. Grades may predict grades, but they fail to predict tolerance of stress, endurance, creativity, or ability to apply what has been learned in the field.

IV. ADDITIONAL READINGS: HISTORICAL ANALYSES, ARGUMENTS, RESEARCH REPORTS

Many of the following entries are self-explanatory; a few warrant a more in-depth review.

76. BECKER, HOWARD, GREER, BLANCHE, and HUGHES, EVERETT. *Making the Grade: The Academic Side of College Life.* New York: John Wiley and Son, 1968 (?) This research team studied the behavior of students at a large midwestern university and through a variety of data-collecting procedures have developed a descriptive analysis of how grades influence the university. Their research uncovered an underlying approach to education which colors almost every aspect of education. They call it the "grade point perspective." It has four characteristics: 1. To remain in the system depends on grades; also to obtain a variety of other goals requires the maintenance of an acceptable grade point. 2. To be perceived as mature within the system depends on your ability to produce grades of a high quality. 3. All other rewards are secondary to grades; like money, it can buy your way to most anything. 4. Grades control energy expenditure since without them all other

goals in academia will be denied. (p. 33-4)

For example, they help direct social life since they are a prime (p. 50) criterion for acceptance into sororities and fraternities, which are the prestigeful social groups on campus. Furthermore, the authors see grades placing students in subordinate positions in the learning equation. The student learns to restrict his behavior and academic performance. Teachers call for open communication and intellectual honesty, but they receive carefully screened behaviors and help develop dependency rather than self-sufficiency. (p. 90) A few quotes from intensive student interviews lay clear the problems posed by the "grade point perspective."

"I don't think about classes. I've got one class where the fellow lectures about one set of things and then gives us an exam on a completely different set of things out of the book. I really don't think I'm going to go to that class anymore. I mean what's the sense of going there and taking notes if he's going to ask questions straight out of the book?" (p. 98)

Another student added:

"The grading systems are so cockeyed around here you can't tell what's going on. One guy does it this way and another guy does it that way and, as I say, the only thing you can do with some courses is get in there and memorize a lot of facts . . . and then you go in and take the final exam and you put it all down on the paper, everything you've memorized, and then you forget it. You walk out of the class and your mind is purged. Perfectly clean. There's nothing in it." (p. 60)

77. CAIN, W. A. "Trends in Marking and Grading." *Texas Outlook*, 1936, 20 #5

This report summarizes the major issues in grading during

the 1930's and a view of some of the changes proposed to reduce the mechanical approach to grading developed during the previous fifteen years.

78. CHAMBERLIN, DEAN, CHAMBERLIN, ENID STRAW, DROUGHT, NEAL E., and SCOTT, WILLIAM E. *Adventures in American Education: Did They Succeed in College?* New York: Harper & Brothers, 1942

Back in the early years of the 1930's college entrance requirements were so rigid and inflexible that for all intents and purposes a secondary school was dictated to in its curriculum or its students would have no opportunity for admissions. Innovation was particularly difficult under such conditions. It was during this period that a vast educational experiment was designed to help determine whether, in fact, students who did not experience the rigid curricular program of the day (four years of a foreign language, particular math and English courses, etc.) could succeed in college and compete on an equal basis with students trained in a more formalized program.

The eight-year study focused on nearly 1500 high school seniors who were allowed entrance into college, not on the basis of particular unit patterns, content *or grades,* but rather based on the recommendations of their principals and other noncurricular requirements of the college of their choice. In 1932, 300 colleges agreed that students from thirty high schools would be set free of traditional academic requirements. The experimental student group was matched with non-participating students according to sex, race, age, religious affiliation, size and type of secondary school, geographic location, socio-economic background, family interests and scholastic aptitude. It was one of the most carefully controlled experiments ever created. Results: While the experimental group did not, as some progressives had hoped, set the college world on fire, they did do as well as or better than the matched control sample undertaking the more traditional program and being directed by grades and particular unit programs. One could not differentiate between the two groups as far as college grades, honors or extra-curricular participation went. The experimentals did slightly better in terms of being perceived as more intellectually curious, more objective in their thinking, appreciative of the arts, and they were judged more resourceful in meeting new situations. It was clearly substantiated that the experimentals without the rigid grading and subject orientation were as well or better prepared for college. The graduates of the experimental schools earned grades which were slightly higher (consistently so) than those in the comparison group. It was thought that they would not earn as high grades in college since they had been taught to study in terms of interest and not in relation to competitive grades. (pp. 22-24) When the data for all the entering classes over all the years of the experiment were compared, the differences in favor of the experimental group had a high level of significance. The probability that the differences in favor of the experimental group were due to chance was less than one in a million. (p. 29)

79. CHANSKY, NORMAN M. "The X-Ray of the School Mark." *The Educational Forum*, March, 1962, pp. 347-52

In a concise and human way, Chansky looks at many of the issues which are causing a reconsideration of grades in schools. For example, he points out that many educators see grades as motivating factors (p. 351). But, research suggests that the downgraded students continue to fail. Furthermore, different students respond to the phenomenon of test anxiety in different ways. For some it is a positive stimulus, while for others it leads to withdrawal and a sense of defeat. Often this stems not from intellectual ability, but rather from past experiences relating to similar situations.

Theoretically, students who receive poor grades on an examination should review materials and retake the examination to determine whether they have internalized the important learnings. However, Chansky points out, since most grades are used to categorize students administratively, there is usually little effort to review or build the skills that have not been learned. Thus, failure is often compounded with later failure and the child never establishes a solid base, since the class moves on whether or, not the child has achieved the needed level of competence.

80. CHANSKY, NORMAN M. "A Note on the Grade Point Average in Research." *Educational and Psychological Measurement,* 1964, 24 #1, pp. 95-99

The author explores the misuses of the familiar GPA by researcher and teacher alike. He focuses on five major points. First, that the grade, the essential ingredient of the GPA, has no inherently stable meaning. Second, capricious judgments and volatile criteria make grade reliability highly suspect. Third, as in the compiling of any average, one loses sight of the extremes. A student may do *A* work in one area and *C* work in another area and come out with a *B* average. His excellence may well be lost. Fourth, seldom are different levels of achievement identified in the grading process (i.e., honors courses from other programs). Finally, grades mean different things to different teachers. Some see grades as representing discrete categories, and others see grades as a relative ordering of achievement. Whether one or the other is used has important implications for the appropriateness of the GPA. Each of these questions is studied at length by Chansky.

81. CROOKS, A. D. "Marks and Marking Systems, A Digest." *Journal of Educational Psychology,* 1933, 27, #4, pp. 259-72
   The rationale for grades and the methodologies used changed dramatically during the decade following the First World War. The article provides a useful synopsis of many of the issues.

82. DEPENCIER, IDA B. "Trends in Reporting Pupil Progress in the Elementary Grades." 1938-49 *Elementary School Journal,* 51, 1951, pp. 519-28
   A useful supplement to Crooks' study (above).

83. GOOD, W. "Should Grades be Abolished?" *Education Digest,* Vol. 2, #4, 1937
   The arguments presented by the author strike a familiar note nearly thirty-five years later.

84. JOHNSON, FRANKLIN "A Study of High School Grades." *School Review,* 19, 1911, pp. 13-24

85. MARSHALL, MAX. *Teaching Without Grades,* Portland, Oregon State University Press, 1969
   A combination of the author's personal experiences with grading, as well as a collection of relevant arguments and research.

86. MCKEACHIE, W. J. "Research on Teaching at the College and University Level," in Nathaniel Lees Gage, *The Handbook of Research on Teaching,* Chicago, Rand McNally, 1963, p. 1142
   Contains several sections relevant to the question of grades and evaluation.

87. National Student Association, Center for Educational Reform, The I.U. Chapter of the New University Conference, *Degrading Education: A Proposal for Abolishing the Grading System*

A pamphlet summarizing much of the research and many of the arguments against grading—very similar to Miller's (App. B, 48) analysis. The pamphlet closes with a proposal for change.

88. ROBERTSON, DON and STEELE, MARION "To Grade Is to Degrade," chapter in *The Halls of Yearning,* Lakewood, California, Andrews Printing Co., Inc., 1969, pp. 41-67
An anti-grade polemic, with a smattering of relevant research. The authors' summary includes 15 arguments against grading. This is worthwhile reading.

89. SMITH, A. and DOBBINS, JOHN, "Marks and Marking Systems," *The Encyclopedia of Educational Research:* Harris, C. W. and Maris, R. L.(editors), New York, MacMillan, 3rd Edition, 1960, pp. 783-791
A thorough review of the trends in marking according to decades beginning with 1910 and ending in 1957.

Appendix B

I. INTRODUCTION

It is important to distinguish between *private* and *public* evaluation.

Private evaluation is an important part of the learning process. It involves the teacher and student working together, sharing information and feedback, identifying strengths and weaknesses, and planning steps toward improved performance. On the elementary and secondary school levels, private evaluation also involves the parents, because they too can play a helpful role in the student's education.

Public evaluation is extrinsic to the learning process. It is the summary data about the student which is made available to parties outside the school and home—particularly to employers and other educational institutions. The data is used to make decisions that subsequently affect the life of the student.

In this appendix, eight alternatives to *public* evaluation are discussed. But it is extremely important to note that, regardless of which public evaluation system is used, there are four ingredients that can and, ideally, should go into *every* system of private evaluation.

A. Clear statement of behavioral objectives, how these will be measured, and what levels of performance will correspond to what specific grades (if grades are used).

B. Meaningful written or oral communication by the teacher to the student, that considers the student's strengths, weaknesses and possible directions for improvement, with respect to the specific course objectives.

C. Student self-evaluation of strengths, weaknesses and directions for improvement, both with respect to the teacher's objectives and with respect to the student's own learning goals.

D. Time for the teacher and student to read each other's evaluations and engage in a dialogue based on this sharing of perceptions.

These recommendations are discussed in greater detail below. But it is worth repeating here that these four aspects of evaluation can significantly aid the learning process, no matter what one's *public* evaluation orientation may be.

Three other points of clarification are in order.

Presenting the eight methods of public evaluation as separate alternatives can be misleading. In reality, many schools combine these methods—often incorporating two or more of the approaches into their own, unique system.

Some of the eight alternatives are system-wide approaches to grading and evaluation. Others are used only by individual teachers in their own classrooms. Most can be used both by individual teachers and an entire school.

The appendix discusses the most frequently used public grading and evaluation systems. There are others. There are also many ways that schools adapt the alternatives described below.

II. ALTERNATIVES TO TRADITIONAL GRADING

A. *Written Evaluations*

1. *Description*

The teacher uses *all* the letters of the alphabet to evaluate the students' work. These evaluations periodically are sent to parents, kept on file in the school and eventually sent to colleges and employers.

Frequently, teachers are provided with a form to guide them in their written evaluations. Such a form might have spaces for the teacher to discuss "strengths," "weaknesses" and "recommendations for improvement." Or it might have a more detailed breakdown of various aspects of a subject, e.g., reading, writing, discussion skills, etc.

Teacher's written evaluations are sometimes combined with the student's written self-evaluation, and both become part of the student's record and are sent to colleges and employers. When a *checklist* form of grading is used, there is often room for the teacher's additional comments. This would be a form of written evaluation.

One school has teachers send out evaluations throughout the year, rather than at specific marking periods. They also provide equal space for the parents' written response.[1]

2. *Advantages*

a. These evaluations are much more helpful to the students than letter or number grades. They have an educational value.

b. Written evaluations are much more meaningful to parents and admissions officers.

c. They encourage the teacher to think more about each student as an individual, rather than as a set of numbers in the grade book.

d. The school with on-going evaluation and parent response says their system encourages on-going attention to student needs, better school-community relations and parental responses which help the teachers write more meaningful evaluations.

3. *Disadvantages*

a. Written evaluations allow teachers to be even more subjective than usual in evaluating students. Teachers might unconsciously minimize the strengths and focus on the weaknesses of students they dislike. Test scores averaged out into a letter grade, in some ways, prevent this kind of subjectivity.

b. Not all teachers know how to write meaningful, helpful individualized evaluations. Some teachers will rely on vague terms like "excellent," "fair," "poor," "needs improvement," "good worker" and so on; their evaluations will be no more meaningful than letter grades.

c. This is a much more time-consuming method of evaluation for teachers.

d. Written evaluations create extra work for the school's records office.

B. *Self-Evaluation*

1. *Description*

There is a need to distinguish between self-evaluation and self-grading. In a formal system of self-evaluation, the student evaluates his own progress, either in writing or in a conference with the teacher. In a system of self-grading, the student determines his own grade. Presumably self-grading cannot take place without prior self-evaluation. On the other hand, some schools have self-evaluation, but no self-grading.

An English department in a Michigan high school has its students write out their own evaluations each quarter. These evaluations then go to the teacher who writes his own comments and reactions to the self-evaluation, if he desires. These evaluations are then sent to the parents and included in the student's permanent records. There are no grades. The student's self-grade can be combined with the teacher's grade for him and the two averaged out to determine the recorded grade. Peer evaluations can be included. Sometimes forms for self-evaluations are devised to guide the student's self-appraisal.

In some settings, students are given freedom to determine many of their educational goals and the means to achieve them. In these cases, students evaluate their progress toward their own goals.[2] Where educational goals and activities are determined by the teacher, self-evaluation implies that students evaluate their progress toward the teacher's goals. Even here, students can help establish the criteria for evaluation, so they can more meaningfully evaluate themselves according to agreed upon criteria.

2. *Advantages*

a. It is an important learning experience for students to evaluate their own strengths and weaknesses.

b. Most teachers who use self-evaluation and self-grading report that students are very fair and objective and often harder on themselves than the teacher would be.

c. Self-evaluation might tend to encourage students to want and teachers to allow students more responsibility for setting educational goals and means of achieving them.

3. *Disadvantages*

a. Initially, students may take the "experiment" of self-evaluation and self-grading very seriously, BUT once the novelty wears off, they may give less thought to their self-evaluation and grade. There is some research to show that, over time, students' self-grades become less accurate.[3]

b. When students respect their teachers they want to grade and evaluate themselves fairly, so the teachers will respect them. When students do not respect or when they dislike their teachers, they might tend to abuse the opportunity of grading themselves.

c. Because of the enormous pressure on students these days to get high grades, self-grading makes honest self-evaluation extremely difficult.

C. *Give Grades But Don't Tell The Students*

1. *Description*

Students receive grades as usual, but they are not told what their grades are. A strong, personalized advising system keeps students apprised of their progress, informs them when they are in danger of failing, and gives them a clear perspective of how they stand in relation to their peers when they are ready to apply to college. At some schools students can find out their grades a certain number of years after they have left the institution.

2. *Advantages*

a. Once the students get used to the idea, tension over grades decreases.

b. Without grades, students stop comparing themselves to one another and begin to shift their focus away from grades and toward learning. Reed College has had this system for over 50 years, and periodic polls show that its alumni are in favor of keeping this system.[4]

3. *Disadvantages*

a. Initially, it might increase tension. For some students, the tension always remains.

b. Although it may reduce tension and help the focus shift away from grades somewhat, many of the problems of traditional grades remain. Even at Reed, there is a movement to introduce pass/fail courses.

D.   *The Contract System*

1. *Description*

There is a need to distinguish between contract grading applied to a whole class and contract grading applied separately to the students.

When applied to a whole class, the contract system means that if the student does a certain *type, quantity* and, ideally, *quality* of work, he will automatically receive a given grade. For example, one teacher made the following contract with his class:

> *Anyone who neither comes to class (type) regularly (quantity) nor turns in all (quantity) the required work (type) will receive an F.*

> *Anyone who only comes to class regularly or only turns in all the required work will receive a D.*

> *Anyone who both comes to class regularly and turns in the required work will receive a C.*

> *Anyone who comes to class regularly, turns in the required work, and the work meets the following criteria (quality) will receive a B.*

> *Anyone who comes to class regularly, turns in the required work that meets the following criteria and does the following extra report will receive an A.*

Sometimes the teacher alone states the terms of the contract. Sometimes they are reached by a group decision. In either case, the same contract applies to the whole class.

Another practice is to have *each student* design his own contract to which the teacher must agree. This use of the contract system implies that students are setting their own goals and ways of reaching those goals, and therefore, different grading procedures will be appropriate for different students. For example, in one social studies class,

Student X might contract to read three books on the United States' political system and write a report on the three books.

Student Y might contract to study the process of how a bill becomes a law and to lead the class in a simulated exercise that would help the class to understand this process better.

Student Z might contract to work two afternoons a week in the campaign headquarters of a local political candidate.

Since each contract calls for a very different *type* of activity than the others, each contract needs to include its own agreement as to how the sudent's grade will be determined. One of the grading variables in this situation will be *who* will do the evaluating. In the case of student X, the teacher might be the sole judge of the grade. For student Y, the class' feedback on the simulated exercise might play a part in the grade. And the local candidate might evaluate the work of student Z. But in all cases, the method of evaluation is decided upon jointly by student and teacher and stated clearly in the original, written contract.

In some classes, the *type* and *quantity* of work are the only components of the contract. Ideally, a contract should also include a statement of how the *quality* of the work will be judged, what criteria will be used and what levels of proficiency are necessary to earn a given grade. To do this adequately requires use of the "mastery approach" toward grading, which is discussed in the next section.

2. *Advantages*

   a. Much of the anxiety is eliminated from the grading process because the student knows, from the beginning of the year, exactly what he has to do to get the grade he wants.

b. To the extent the teacher specifies the quantity and quality required for each grade, some of the subjectivity is eliminated from the grading process, and students have a clearer idea of what is expected of them.

c. The contract system, when applied to students individually, encourages diversity in the classroom, encourages students to set and follow their own learning goals and decreases unhealthy competition.

3. *Disadvantages*

a. The *quantity* of work is easily over-emphasized in contracts and tends to become the sole basis for a grade. To use an extreme example, one English teacher stipulated that five-page compositions would receive an *A*, four-page compositions would receive a *B*, and so on. When the quantity of work becomes the sole criterion for the grade, the grade loses its meaning.

b. It is difficult to find creative ways to measure the *quality* of the different types of work students may contract to do.

c. There is a danger that teachers will be too ambiguous in attempting to state the *qualitative* distinctions between grades. To say that work of "excellent" quality will receive an *A*, work of "good" quality will receive a *B*, and so on, is no different than the ambiguous and subjective criteria we presently employ.

E. *The Mastery Approach or Performance Curriculum*[5]
(Five-Point System)

1. *Description*

The mastery approach is not only a different method of

grading, but an entirely different approach toward teaching and learning. It may be practiced by one class or by an entire department or subject area. In a sense, it is not an alternative to traditional grading; rather, it *is* the traditional grading system, done effectively.

The mastery approach begins with the teacher deciding what his operational or behavioral objectives are for his students, that is, what exactly he wants them to be able to *do* as a result of their learnings.[6] He then organizes these learnings into units of study and arranges the units in a logical sequence, each unit serving as a necessary or logical building block to the unit succeeding it. Then the teacher determines how he will measure the extent to which his students have mastered the body of knowledge and skills in each of the units.

For each unit, the teacher designates levels of mastery or proficiency. Thus, if a math teacher wants his students to be able to solve a quadratic equation, he stipulates what the student must do to demonstrate a *C* level of proficiency, what he must do to demonstrate a *B* level of proficiency, and so on.

At the very beginning of the course, the teacher provides the students with all this information—what they are expected to learn, how their learnings will be tested, what the criteria are for the different levels of proficiency and what level of proficiency is required before they can move on to the next part of the course. In addition, he explains to the students what resources are available to help them achieve the levels of mastery they desire.

Students are then free to master the course content in their own fashion. Some students will attend class lectures and discussions. Others will work independently. Many students will utilize the various resources the teacher has provided—learning packages, programmed texts, films, tapes, speakers, field trips, etc.

Each student proceeds at his own pace. One student may take a semester to accomplish what is normally done in a year. Another student may take a year to do a semester's work in a particular subject. Under this system the course is oriented much more to the individual student, and the professor spends most of his time in review seminars and in individual tutoring, rather than in large group lectures.

Students ask to be examined when they think they are ready to move on. Usually, when a student has achieved a *C* level of mastery in one unit of a course, he can choose to go on to the next unit. However, students who want to earn *B* or *A* grades will stay with each unit until they have achieved that level of proficiency. A student may take an exam (a different form each time, of course) over again until he is satisfied with his grade.

Using the mastery approach, several teachers or an entire department can get together and plan their courses sequentially—one course building upon the next. This is sometimes called a performance curriculum, since course credits are no longer determined by the length of *time* a student spends with a given subject ("I had three years of French.") but by the level of *performance* he has achieved in a given area.

Bucknell's Continuous Progress Program is one example of the mastery approach and performance curriculum. Courses as different as biology, philosophy, psychology, physics, religion and education are all involved.[7]

2. *Advantages*

   a. A student's grade becomes more meaningful to him because it is tied to a performance level. In the performance curriculum, grades become more meaningful because, in several different classes, the same grade now means the same thing.

b. Much of the teacher's subjectivity in grading is eliminated.

c. When students know where they are heading, they are likely to get there faster.

d. The focus of this system is on success, not failure.

e. The student has freedom to pursue his own path in mastering the course content.

f. The teacher is held accountable for stating his objectives, providing many resources and helping his students achieve mastery. Sloppy organization and ill-prepared teachers are readily noticeable.

g. In the performance curriculum, the cooperation among teachers can generate better morale and the sharing of resources.

3. *Disadvantages*

a. To utilize the mastery approach properly requires considerable skill on the part of teachers and administrators. Most educators were not trained in this method and a great deal of re-training will be necessary. The funds are not easily available.

b. The performance curriculum somewhat limits a teacher's freedom to run his classes in just his own way. In some cases this might be desirable; in other cases some creative teachers might be hampered.

c. It is possible for teachers to use the mastery approach without allowing students to pursue their own ways of achieving the levels of proficiency. When this happens students might feel, more than many do now, that all their education means is jumping over a series of prescribed hurdles.

d. Even when students have freedom to choose *how* they

will achieve the teacher's goals, the mastery approach discourages them from setting and working toward *their own* goals.

e. The total faculty must be involved in setting up a performance curriculum. The teachers in each subject area would have to carefully study goals and methods and explore new approaches to the subject matter. This could take a very long time and might normally be impossible, since most teachers teach 5 classes, have supervisory duties and are involved in one or more student activities. A long-term grant might be needed to hire additional personnel to free teachers to do the necessary research and curriculum development.

F. *Pass/Fail Grading (P/F)*

1. *Description*

At the beginning of the course, the teacher states his criteria for a passing grade, or else the teacher and students together decide on the criteria for a passing grade. Any student who meets these criteria passes; any student who does not meet these criteria fails. Students have the opportunity to redo failing work to bring it up to passing quality.

Pass/fail is a form of blanket grading, with the blanket grade being a *P*. *P/F* is also a form of the contract system, since the students know that if they meet the teacher's stated criteria for passing, they will automatically receive a *P*. Finally, it is also a form of the mastery approach, since the teacher designates the level of mastery needed to pass the course.

2. *Advantages*

a. Students are more relaxed, less anxious and less competitive.

b. There is a better learning atmosphere. Students feel freer to take risks, disagree with the teacher, and explore the subject in their own way.

c. There is no point to cheating or apple-polishing (except for students in danger of failing).

d. Students still have to meet the teacher's requirements to get the blanket grade, so plenty of work gets done. Freed from the pressures of traditional grading, some students do even more work than usual.

3. *Disadvantages*

   a. Some teachers will use pass/fail grading as an excuse to avoid all evaluation. This deprives the student of potentially helpful feedback.

   b. The passing grade does not distinguish between students of different abilities. Therefore, the grade is meaningless except to connote passing work.

   c. Freed from the pressures of traditional grading, some students do less work than usual.

   d. Just as it is difficult for teachers to distinguish between the different levels of mastery in the performance curriculum, it will be difficult to clearly state and measure the level of mastery needed to earn the passing grade.

   e. The student in danger of failing still labors under all the pressures normally associated with traditional grading. *P/F* is no help to our poorer students.

4. *Note*

   The system of pass/fail grading has two kinds of variations:

   a. *Modified Pass/Fail* which adds one category to denote

outstanding work. This is called Honors/Pass/Fail (*H/P/F*).

b. *Limited Pass/Fail* in which the student may take only *some* of his courses on a pass/fail basis.

The advantages and disadvantages of both of these variations are discussed in detail in Chapter 13.

G.   Credit/No Credit Grading (*CR/NC*)

1. Description

This system works precisely the same way as pass/fail grading, except the two categories are "credit" and "no credit" instead of pass and fail. *CR/NC* also can be practiced on a modified or limited basis. It is important for systems using *CR/NC* to note right in their transcripts that *NC* does *not* connote failing work.

2. Advantages

Same as those for pass/fail but with one additional advantage: "No Credit" does not connote failure; students simply do not get credit for the course. With this fear of an *F* removed from those students on the borderline, they, too, can feel freer from the need to cheat and con their way to a passing grade. It is a small difference, but significant for those on the borderline.

3. Disadvantages

Same as those for pass/fail, except for "e."

H. *Blanket Grading*

1. *Description*

The teacher announces at the beginning of the year that anyone in the class who does the required amount of work will receive the blanket grade. Usually, the grade is *B*. Sometimes classes use the blanket *A* to make a protest statement to the school. Sometimes a blanket *C* is used, as a way of saying to the school, "See, this is how little we care about grades. The focus in this class will be on learning."

If a student's work is of such poor quality that the teacher does not feel justified in giving him the blanket grade, he allows the student to keep trying until the quality improves.

This is a form of contract grading. It is also a form of the mastery approach, since the teacher is saying, "Anyone who achieves this minimum level of mastery will receive the blanket grade."

Blanket grading is used in individual classrooms only; it is never used by a whole school.

2. *Advantages*

Same as those for Pass/Fail Grading.

3. *Disadvantages*

   a. Same as those for Pass/Fail Grading.
   b. Although teachers frequently use blanket grading without any repercussions, this system would violate most school's written or unwritten grading policies and, therefore, be a risk for the teacher.

Notes and References

Notes and References

INTRODUCTION

1. HERBERS, JOHN, "High School Unrest Rises, Alarming U.S. Educators," *New York Times,* May 9, 1969, p. 1

CHAPTER 4

1. CUBBERLEY, ELLWOOD, *The History of Education,* Cambridge, Massachusetts, Houghton Mifflin Company, 1922, pp. 677-708
2. EDWARDS, NEWTON and RICHEY, HERMAN G., *The School in the American Social Order,* Cambridge, Massachusetts, Houghton Mifflin Company, 1947, pp. 386-427
3. HOFSTADTER, RICHARD, MILLER, WILLIAM and AARON, DANIEL, *The American Republic,* New Jersey, Prentice Hall, Inc., 1959, p. 306, *Volume Two*
4. STARCH, DANIEL and ELLIOTT, EDWARD C., "Reliability of the Grading of High School Work in English," *School Review,* Vol. 20, 1912
5. STARCH, DANIEL and ELLIOTT, EDWARD C., "Reliability in Grading Work in Mathematics," *School Review,* Vol. 21, 1913
6. MEYER, MAX F., "Grading of Students," *Science,* Vol. 28, 1908
7. JOHNSON, ROSEWELL H., "The Coefficient Marking System," *The School and Society,* Vol. 7, June, 1918
8. DEARBORN, WALTER F., *School and University Grades,* Madison, University of Wisconsin Press, 1910, reported in *The Encyclopedia of Educational Research,* New York, Macmillan Co., 1960, p. 784
9. RUGG, HAROLD O., "Teachers' Marks and the Reconstruction of the System," *Elementary School Journal,* Vol. 18, May, 1918
10. ROELFS, R. M., "Trends in Junior High School Reporting," *Journal of Educational Research,* Vol. 18, May, 1918
11. MIDDLETON, WARREN, "Some General Trends in Grading Procedures," *Education,* Vol. 54, No. 1, September, 1933
12. WHITTEN, C. W., "Standardizing and Making Uniform Teachers' Marks," *The Sixth Yearbook of the NASSP,* 1922
13. CHAPMAN, H. B., and ASHBAUGH, E. J., "Report Cards in American Cities," *Educational Research Bulletin,* Vol. 4, October, 1925
14. JOHNSON, FRANKLIN, "A Study of High School Grades," *School Review,* Vol. 28, 1920

15. ROGERS, FREDERICK R., "Education Versus the Marking System," *Education,* Vol. 52, May, 1952

16. PRESSEY, S. I., "Fundamental Misconceptions Involved in Current Marking Systems," *School and Society,* Vol. 21, June, 1925

17. WETZEL, WILLIAM, "The Use of the Normal Curve of Distribution in Estimating Student Marks," *School Review,* Vol. 20, 1912

18. CREW, H. "President's Address—Annual Meeting." *American Association of University Professors,* B. 16, reported in *Encyclopedia of Educational Research,* New York, Macmillan Co., 1960, p. 786

19. GOOD, WARREN, "Should Grades Be Abolished?" *Education Digest,* Vol. 2, No. 4, 1937

20. HECK, ARCH O., "Contributions of Research to the Classification, Promotion, Marking and Certification," reported in *The Science Movement in Education,* part II of the 27th Annual NSSE Yearbook, 1938

21. EBEL, ROBERT L. "Basic Considerations in Grading the Achievement of College Students," address given before the Fall Conference of the Florida State University Faculty, September 10, 1956

22. BERMAN, SAMUEL, "Philadelphia Progress Reports," *The School Executive,* June, 1941 (authors' additions to Berman's data)

23. BERMAN, SAMUEL, "Revising the Junior High School Report Card," *The National Association of Secondary School Principals,* Vol. 27, No. 115, January, 1943 (authors' additions to Berman's data)

24. ROELFS, *op. cit.*

25. HILL, GEORGE, "The Report Card in Present Practice," *Education Methods,* Vol. 15, No. 3, December, 1935, p. 19

CHAPTER 5

1. In 1968, Brian Patrick McGuire was graduated from the University of California at Berkeley with the highest grade-point average in the College of Letters and Science. Mr. McGuire was invited to deliver a speech at the annual Phi Beta Kappa dinner, at which time he advocated the elimination of the traditional grading system. This chapter is based on Mr. McGuire's article "The Grading Game," which appeared in *Today's Education,* March, 1969. About two pages of MacIntyre's speech are composed of McGuire's own words.

2. HOLT, JOHN. *How Children Fail,* New York, Dell Publishing Co., 1964, p. 168

CHAPTER 7

1. ROTHNEY, JOHN W. M., *What Research Says to the Teacher* (about)

Evaluating and Reporting Pupil Progress, Washington, D. C., National Education Association, 1955, p. 13

2. ROBERTSON, DON and MARION STEELE. *The Halls of Yearning,* Lakewood, California, Andrews Printing Co., Inc., 1969, p. 51

3. In industry, it was found that employees would more readily ask help of their supervisors if the supervisors weren't also responsible for evaluation. See Ross, I. C. *Role Specialization in Supervision,* unpublished doctoral dissertation, Columbia Univ., 1956 (Dissertation Abstracts, 1956, 17, 2701-2702)

4. KNOWLTON, JAMES Q. and HAMERLYNCK, LEO A., "Perception of Devient Behavior: A Study of Cheating," *Journal of Educational Psychology,* December, 1967, pp. 379-385

5. CANNING, R. R. "Does an Honor System Reduce Classroom Cheating?" *Journal of Experimental Education,* 23:291-96 (June, 1956)

6. RENO, RAYMOND H. "The Teacher as Grader," address presented before Opening General Session of the Hartford Regional TEPS Conference, January 8, 1968

7. Zipper and Warsaw, Queens College *Phoenix,* October 11, 1966

8. FEIFFER, JULES, *Village Voice,* March 7, 1969, p. 4

9. RUSSELL, NORMAN H. *American Association of University Professors Bulletin,* Winter, 1966, p. 414

10. To avoid embarrassment to the Dean of Faculty who wrote this letter, the authors have chosen to withhold the particulars on this *very* real letter.

11. Want Ads, Temple University *News,* November 21, 1969, p. 7

12. Personal Department, *Village Voice,* New York City, April 17, 1969, p. 61

13. For an excellent presentation of the advantages and methodologies of group problem solving, see NORMAN R. F. MAIER, *Problem Solving Discussions and Conferences: Leadership Methods and Skills,* New York, McGraw-Hill Book Company, 1963

CHAPTER 8

1. Ingles' story is based on an experience of Kathy Davis, former Pennsylvania High School student, related in a personal communication to one of the authors, 1969.

2. JOANNE MALLAS wrote this for a class assignment when she was a junior at the New Lincoln School, New York City, 1969

3. BOGIN, MICHAEL and MADDEN, ROBERT, Queens College *Phoenix,* Tuesday, April 13, 1965. The letter in this chapter is a condensation and slight adaptation of the original.

CHAPTER 12

The 70 references in this chapter can be found in Appendix A: An Annotated Bibliography of Research on Grading.

CHAPTER 13

1. GAUSS, JOHN, in *Saturday Review*, July 21, 1962, reprinted from *Phi Delta Kappan*, January, 1962
2. ROBERTSON and STEELE, *op. cit.*, p. 53
3. "Pass-Fail Study Committee Report to the Senate," Washington, D. C., Phi Beta Kappa, 1970
4. ROBERTSON and STEELE, *op. cit.*, p. 60
5. STANDEL, STEPHEN, Assistant Principal, John Dewey High School, personal communication to authors, 1969
6. The Lewis-Wadhams School, Elizabethtown, New York, surveyed 30 colleges in this manner. The overwhelming response of the colleges was that there would be absolutely no prejudice against students applying from a school that did not give grades. These students would be judged solely on the basis of the other information (SAT scores, recommendations, student self-evaluations, etc.) which the school provided.
7. "Colleges are sympathetic to that outook [that grades are too *un*-specific to be useful]. When Murray Road seniors file their applications, they send self-evaluations and teachers' evaluations in place of the usual grades and class rank. Only two large universities have refused to consider the applications—because their computers couldn't process them. A number of prestigious colleges and universities have assured the schools that teacher evaluations will be an adequate replacement for class rank and grades." SILBERMAN, ARLENE. "Bold New Directions for U.S. High Schools," *Reader's Digest*, August, 1970, p. 89

CHAPTER 14

1. The Committee's Recommendation is, in some ways, similar to that adopted by Brown University. This is discussed in an excellent article, "How and Why Brown Broke the Curriculum Mold," *College Management*, October, 1969, pp. 22-33
2. The suggestions made in letters *a* through *f* above are excerpted from the "Report of the Superintendent's Marking-Grading Committee," Great Neck, New York Public Schools, February, 1970. The report recommends a complete shift from traditional grading to credit/no credit grading, to begin with the seventh grade and

include one additional grade each year until 1975, at which time credit/no credit grading would exist throughout the secondary schools. The principal of Great Neck North Senior High School, Mr. M. Elliot Noyes, is a member of the committee and a strong supporter of the proposal for change.

APPENDIX B

1. Shelbourne, Vermont middle school; John Winton, Principal.
2. ROGERS, CARL R. *Freedom to Learn,* Columbus, Ohio, Charles E. Merrill Publishing Co., Inc., 1969, pp. 91, 142, 201
3. See RUSSELL, DAVID H. "What Does Research Say About Self-Evaluation?" *Journal of Educational Research,* Vol. 46, No. 8 (April, 1953) pp. 561-573 for a summary of major findings at that time. These studies tend to support the view that student self-evaluations are usually invalid measures of achievement and personality adjustment. However, in all those studies, students were not trained or experienced in self-evaluation. If schools systematically encouraged on-going self-evaluation, one might hypothesize more valid results.
4. Information available to the public from the Registrar, Reed College, Portland, Oregon
5. See BLOOM, BENJAMIN S. "Learning for Mastery," in UCLA's *Evaluation Comment,* Vol. I, No. 2, May, 1968
6. For a brief, easy, enjoyable and excellent presentation on "behavioral objectives" and how to build them into an instructional program, see MAGER, ROBERT F. *Preparing Instructional Objectives,* Palo Alto, California, Fearon Publishers, Inc. 1962
7. MOORE, J. WILLIAM, "A Program for Systematic Instructional Improvement," *Audiovisual Instruction,* February, 1970, pp. 28-30